This Is your Day for a Miracle

BENNY HINN

This Is your Day for a Miracle

Creation House
Strang Communications Company
600 Rinehart Road
Lake Mary, FL 32746
Fax: 407-333-7100

Unless otherwise noted, all Scripture quotations are
from *THE MESSAGE.* Copyright © 1993, 1994, 1995. Used
by permission of NavPress Publishing Group.

Scripture quotations marked KJV are from the
King James Version of the Bible.

Scripture quotations marked NIV are from the
Holy Bible, New International Version. Copyright © 1973,
1978, 1984, International Bible Society.
Used by permission.

Scripture quotations marked NKJV are from the
New King James Version of the Bible. Copyright © 1979,
1980, 1982 by Thomas Nelson Inc., publishers.
Used by permission.

*Dedicated in loving memory to
Kathryn Kuhlman, whom God used
greatly to touch my life.*

Acknowledgments

First of all I want to thank every person who took the time to tell their testimony. I share in the excitement of your miracle and thank you for allowing me to use it to encourage others.

I am also grateful to the editors of Creation House for helping me research the medical aspects of these stories.

Special thanks to Neil Eskelin for helping me put words to paper, and to Don Colbert, M.D.; Gene Koziara, M.D.; and Randal Eha, D.C.; for reviewing medical documentation.

Finally I'd like to say how grateful I am to Sue Langford and the Medical Follow-up Department of our ministry. Their hard work allows stories like these to go out and bless thousands of people.

Contents

Foreword

AS A MEDICAL doctor, I was taught in school to logically arrive at a diagnosis, using the patient's history, the physical exam, lab studies, X-rays and other medical tests deemed necessary. When a patient receives treatment, there is an expectation for a certain response. This entire process is based on logic in order to arrive at a correct diagnosis.

During the past ten years of my medical practice, I have seen many people miraculously healed. Such a healing often defies all logical explanation. Logic can actually hinder one's healing if it gets in the way of faith because we receive from God through faith.

I pray that the wonderful, miraculous testimonies in this book will inspire your faith and enable you to receive your miracle. Each testimony features documentation which supports the patient's healing.

While studying at Oral Roberts University, I saw many miracles happen under the great ministry of Oral Roberts. One of those miracles was a healing in my own body. During medical school I suffered a heat stroke and nearly died. Due to the damage caused by the high temperatures in my body during the heat stroke, I was hospitalized for nearly two weeks experiencing acute renal failure and muscle necrosis of my legs. (Necrosis means actual death of the muscle.) I was then told that I may never walk again.

My legs shrank down so small that my arms appeared to be thicker than my legs. A muscle biopsy confirmed the muscle necrosis. Unshaken in our faith, my wife, family and friends united themselves in prayer and agreement, and I had a miraculous recovery.

I have been a member of World Outreach Center under Pastor Benny Hinn since 1984 and have traveled extensively with the crusade team both in the United States and abroad. I never cease to be amazed at the mighty moves of God and at the great healings that occur during the crusades.

The majority of these healings occur during the worship times when thousands of voices are raised to the Lord in one accord. At these times, the presence of the Holy Spirit fills the entire meeting hall, and one can tangibly feel it. In this great atmosphere of worship, the Holy Spirit is able to minister to individuals.

Some people are healed as they take steps of faith. They may raise their arms or stand and walk when they couldn't do so before. I have also heard many testimonies of people receiving healing as they prayed for another person during the worship times. Still others receive a miracle even before the service begins as crusade helpers or others are praying in agreement with them.

I am also amazed at the number of miracles that occur during Pastor Hinn's TV broadcast. Even as people watch Pastor Hinn's old videotapes the anointing is still so strong that healings occur.

It is my sincere desire that every person reading this book will allow the Holy Spirit to minister to them and that they will expect to receive a miracle. When we receive a miracle, it's also vitally important to follow God's health laws. Our bodies are the temples of the Holy Ghost, and we should not put drugs, alcohol or cigarettes into them or eat excessive amounts of fatty or sweet foods. We should also exercise and maintain our temples. When properly cared for, God designed the human body to live a long, healthy life.

While I was reading this book and reviewing the medical documentation associated with each individual miracle, at times the anointing would be so strong that I would stop reading and begin to praise and worship the Lord for the great miracles that only He could perform. Many healings are so touching that you will find it difficult to hold back the tears. This book will fill you with hope as you read about people being healed of cancer, heart disease, orthopedic problems and other illnesses.

God specializes in performing miracles. The individuals in this book discovered that fact for themselves. Expect the miracle of healing to affect your life and the lives of the people around you. Live your life in praise to the awesome, miracle-working Great Physician. This is *your* day for a miracle.

Donald Colbert, M.D.
Orlando, Florida

1

Yes, I Believe

"WHY ME?" I asked myself, frozen with fear. "Why would they ask a twenty-four-year-old preacher from Canada to speak at an event like this?" My knees were beyond knocking, and my throat was so dry I could hardly swallow.

I was backstage at the beautiful Carnegie Music Hall in Pittsburgh, Pennsylvania, ready to be introduced to those assembled in the packed auditorium. They had gathered that day in February 1977 for a memorial service in honor of Kathryn Kuhlman. The famed evangelist had passed away just one year earlier, and now an overflow crowd had gathered for this special event. Even her choir had reassembled to honor her that evening in the city where she held weekly services for more than twenty-five years.

Earlier that afternoon, after arriving from Toronto, I went to the offices of the Kathryn Kuhlman Foundation and met Jimmy McDonald, the great gospel singer who had been with Miss Kuhlman for years, and Maggie Hartner, Kathryn's loyal assistant. Before that time I had only said a passing hello to them at one of the miracle services in Pittsburgh and had never been formally introduced.

"We've heard about your ministry and are happy you could be here for this special day," said Maggie.

"How had she heard about me?" I wondered, since I was relatively unknown outside of Toronto.

I was amazed they had asked me to participate. I was even more surprised when I learned the full scope of the service that was planned. "We are going to show the film of Miss Kuhlman's meeting in Las Vegas, and then we want you to conduct a healing service."

"A healing service?" I exclaimed. "Are you sure?"

I felt so out of place. I knew it would be awkward for me to walk out after the film with people thinking, "Who is this unknown fellow up there praying for the sick?" I could just hear them saying, "Does he think he's going to replace Kathryn?"

"Maggie," I said, "I feel extremely uncomfortable with the idea of praying for the sick at a memorial service. Wouldn't it be better if I just told how Miss Kuhlman's ministry influenced my life?"

Jimmy McDonald, who is now one of our crusade soloists, agreed. "Maybe he's right. Should we really have a healing service?"

A very strong-willed Maggie insisted. "That's what I want, and that is what will happen." She asked Jimmy to introduce me.

I Couldn't Move

Now, from my vantage point behind the curtains, my eyes were wandering nervously as the crowd filled the hall — one of the most beautiful auditoriums in America with ornate gold carvings and exquisitely painted balconies. I continued to wonder, "Why me?" as I found a place where I could see the film.

The lights went down, a hush came over the crowd and the film started. It was powerful. It had been filmed at a service in the packed Las Vegas Convention Center, held in May 1975 — the only time Miss Kuhlman had personally allowed one of her meetings to be captured on film. The five-hour service had been condensed to ninety dynamic minutes.

I had seen the film previously, and my stomach was in knots. "How can I ever follow this?" I wondered. Then, a few minutes before the conclusion, Jimmy motioned for me to go to the back of the platform with him.

Standing in the darkness, he told me, "When the lights are raised I will walk out, introduce you and begin singing, 'Jesus, Jesus, There's Just Something About That Name.'" He asked me to come to the front of the platform once the audience joined him in that chorus.

In his introduction Jimmy said things I never knew — like the fact that before Miss Kuhlman died, she told her staff that she had heard about my ministry and asked them to help me any way they could.

The more Jimmy elaborated about me the more nervous I became. When he began to sing, I looked out from behind the curtains, petrified. Only two years earlier, at the age of twenty-two, I had preached my first sermon. And now this.

I was so frightened I literally could not move.

Jimmy McDonald sang the chorus a second time — and a third. Finally, giving me one last cue, he told the audience, "We're going to sing the song for the last time as Benny Hinn comes out onto the platform."

An usher, sensing the situation, gave me a push, and I timidly walked onto the stage — turning pale with trepidation. Jimmy gave me a relieved look that said, "What took you so long?"

He handed me the microphone and left me there alone. I could feel every eye in the crowd staring at me.

The musicians had changed the song and were playing softly in the background, but my mind was a total blank. All I could say was, "Let's sing that again."

Well, I tried, but because they had switched keys I couldn't find the right note and began singing the chorus by myself in a very high pitch. My voice was squeaking, and I was totally embarrassed.

A few moments later I just broke down and cried. I looked up at the ceiling and said, "Lord, I cannot do it."

At that instant the Lord spoke to me and replied,

"I'm glad you cannot, because I will."

I spoke briefly of Kathryn Kuhlman's dramatic impact on my life. Just before Christmas 1973, I traveled on a chartered bus from Toronto to attend one of her Friday morning services at Pittsburgh's First Presbyterian Church. There were testimonies of healings for tumors, arthritis, headaches and more. But I had never heard anyone talk about the Holy Spirit as she did. With her eyes ablaze, she began to sob, pleading, "Please." She seemed to stretch out the word, "Plee-ease don't grieve the Holy Spirit!"

Then I told of how the red-haired evangelist said, "Don't you understand? He's all I've got. He's my closest, most personal, most intimate, most beloved Friend."

I shared how I returned to my home that night and lay on my bed desperate to understand what the woman in the long, flowing white dress had meant. I thought, "I want what Kathryn Kuhlman's got." That same night the Holy Spirit came into my room and, for the first time, I entered into a personal relationship with the Spirit that transformed my life.

After I told that story, I began to minister in the music hall, and suddenly the power of God descended. Miracles began to happen. The people were ecstatic, yet no one was more amazed than me.

Miss Kuhlman had the greatest team in the world. When Maggie, Ruth Fisher and others sensed the anointing of the Spirit they moved into the aisles and spoke with people who were being healed. Before long the platform was filled with those sharing their remarkable testimonies.

Kathryn Kuhlman was no longer with us, but God's Spirit was still very much present.

At the invitation of the Kathryn Kuhlman Foundation, I returned the following month to the Soldier's and Sailor's Memorial Hall and held monthly services in Pittsburgh for the next four years. I was also humbled to frequently host her syndicated radio program and to travel to major cities in the U.S. and Canada where we showed the film and conducted healing services that touched the lives of thousands.

Why I Believe

I have recently been listening again to Miss Kuhlman's tapes titled "The Gifts of the Spirit." My mind continues to flash back to the days in the early 1970s when, night after night in my Toronto bedroom, I listened to her quiet, captivating voice on WWVA, the powerful fifty-thousand-watt radio station in Wheeling, West Virginia. Then, as often as possible, I journeyed to Pittsburgh to attend unforgettable Friday morning services she conducted until just before her passing.

I have listened to her tapes many times in the last twenty years, yet it seems as if the messages were preached just yesterday. I am seeing God do the exact same things now in our crusades. I find myself saying again and again, "Yes. Yes. The Spirit is still moving! The Lord is still healing!"

Please don't misunderstand; I don't believe in miracles because of Kathryn Kuhlman or because of what I experienced in her meetings. Frankly, I have believed in miracles for as long as I can remember — even before I became a Christian.

I was born in Israel, a country that to me is a miracle in itself. In school, the Catholic nuns taught me from the Bible how Jesus healed the sick and cast out demons and that miracles still happen.

I grew up in the town of Jaffa, near the Mediterranean Sea, where people accepted the reality of the supernatural, though they did not know God. Many practiced an ancient custom of building a small fire, placing incense on it and walking across the flame. That was supposed to keep demonic spirits away.

When I became a born-again believer, however, I realized that it is God, not man's actions, who brings healing and deliverance.

Today there are three great reasons that cause me to know God still performs miracles.

1. I believe in miracles because the Word declares it.

Scripture tells me, "Surely he took up our infirmities and carried our sorrows" (Is. 53:4, NIV). Jesus declared, "They shall lay hands on the sick, and they shall recover" (Mark 16:18, KJV).

2. I believe in miracles because my experience confirms it.

From early childhood I was afflicted with a severe stutter. The smallest amount of social pressure or nervousness triggered my stammering, and it was almost unbearable. Then on December 7, 1974, in Oshawa,

Ontario, when I first stood in a pulpit to preach, something marvelous occurred. The instant I opened my mouth I felt something touch my tongue and loosen it, and I began to proclaim God's Word with absolute fluency. The stuttering was gone. All of it. And it has never returned.

3. I believe in miracles because the evidence verifies it.

I have seen people walk out of wheelchairs, throw away hearing aids and describe how tumors disappeared. I tell them often, "Go to your doctor. Have your miracle verified and send us the report."

Friends, the evidence is in. The files in our offices are filled with before-and-after medical reports showing God's healing power.

The Source of Miracles

People who like to label me a "divine healer" are often surprised when they come to our crusades and find that we do not have healing lines. I rarely pray for individuals. Instead, I believe God has clearly called me to bring people into His presence where the Holy Spirit can do His work. When I hold a healing service, the people come to the platform to praise God for a miracle that has already taken place.

Yes, there are examples in Scripture when Jesus personally laid hands on those who were sick, but as the Lord was walking past a blind man on the road to Jericho, Jesus merely spoke to him and healing came.

He said, "Receive thy sight: thy faith hath saved thee" (Luke 18:42, KJV).

I remember Miss Kuhlman saying in her meetings, "If you believe that I, an individual, have any power to heal, you are dead wrong. I have no healing power whatsoever. All I can do is point you to the Way — I can lead you to the Great Physician, and I can pray, but the rest is left with you and God."

Do I believe in medical science? Absolutely. God uses everything at His disposal in the healing process — including physicians. As Miss Kuhlman stated, "A doctor has the power and ability to set a bone, but he must wait for divine power to heal. A surgeon can skillfully perform the most difficult of operations; he may be a master with a scalpel, using every facet of his well-trained intellect; yet he must wait for a higher power to do the actual healing — for no mere human being has ever been given the power to heal."

Every day I hear remarkable accounts of people who have been miraculously healed. As people testify at our crusades and conferences and send us thousands of letters, I stand in awe at what the Lord is doing.

We need to remember, however, that what we call extraordinary is ordinary to God. What we call supernatural is natural to the Lord. And what we call a miracle is an everyday occurrence to the one who spoke the world into existence and breathed life into man.

I believe that same God has a miracle for you!

2

Are Miracles for Today?

BENNY, WE BELIEVE God wants to use you in a special way," my friend Jim Poynter told me — speaking for a group of ministers who asked me to conduct some meetings in Willowdale, a suburb of Toronto. "We're going to rent the cafeteria of a public school and leave the rest up to the Lord."

It was February 1975, just two months after I had first shared my testimony at a small church in Oshawa, Ontario.

The ministers were taking quite a chance. I certainly had no track record as an evangelist. I was simply a young man who had turned my life completely over to the Lord. The small crowd gathered in the cafeteria that night did not know what to expect, and neither did I.

Someone recently asked, "Pastor Benny, when did you know that healing would be part of your ministry?"

I didn't know what God had in mind for my ministry, even though I was healed of a life-long stuttering habit when I gave my testimony in a church for the first time. At Willowdale we conducted several services before I felt led to ask those who needed a healing touch from God to come forward for prayer. In those days I formed a "healing line" and personally prayed for those individuals who requested prayer. The Lord began to do some marvelous things.

"I think we need to find a larger auditorium and continue these services," said one of the sponsoring ministers. To my delight we moved to Georges Vanier Secondary School where I had once been a student. It had been in that same building, at a student-led early morning prayer meeting, that I asked Christ to come into my heart.

In May 1975, the Lord impressed me to do something I had never done before. By that time our services were being held in the beautiful fellowship hall of St. Paul's Anglican Church in Toronto. During one service with about three hundred people present, I looked up into the balcony and obeyed what the Lord was telling me. "Someone with a leg problem is being healed," I declared.

No one stood up, so I repeated the words. "Someone with a leg problem is being healed right now! Please stand up."

About a minute later a young lady with long red-
dish hair stood to her feet in the balcony and began
to make her way to the platform. "It's me!" she
exclaimed. "I have been healed."

From that moment God changed the direction of
the ministry. In service after service, healings began
taking place while the meeting was in progress.
People rejoiced when they heard the testimonies of
those who came forward to declare what God was
doing. The crowds grew and grew, and we soon
moved to the 3,200-seat main sanctuary of St. Paul's
Anglican Church.

The Power of Unity

People often ask, "Do I need to attend a crusade to
receive my healing?"

Absolutely not. We serve a sovereign God who acts
according to *His* schedule, not *ours*. But after years of
ministry I am convinced that the coming together of
God's people in a crusade produces an atmosphere of
faith. When believers gather in unity — whether it be
two, two thousand or two hundred thousand — faith
is present. Jesus made that point clear when He
stated: "For where two or three are gathered together
in my name, there am I in the midst of them" (Matt.
18:20, KJV).

When Moses was leading the children of Israel
through the wilderness and they were under attack,
he said to Joshua, "Choose some of our men and go
out to fight the Amalekites. Tomorrow I will stand on
top of the hill with the staff of God in my hands" (Ex.
17:9, NIV).

During the battle Moses did as God instructed and

"as long as Moses held up his hands, the Israelites were winning, but whenever he lowered his hands, the Amalekites were winning" (v. 11).

What happened when Moses' hands grew tired? Scripture records that "Aaron and Hur held his hands up — one on one side, one on the other — so that his hands remained steady till sunset" (v. 12). The Amalekite army was defeated.

Where there is unity, God's power is not only present, but *multiplied*.

Before Jesus ascended to heaven, He said to His disciples, "And, behold, I send the promise of my Father upon you: but tarry ye in the city of Jerusalem, until ye be endued with power from on high" (Luke 24:49, KJV).

Not only did they follow the Lord's command, but they invited other believers to join them. One hundred and twenty gathered in the upper room and "when the day of Pentecost was fully come, they were all with one accord in one place" (Acts 2:1, KJV).

When did the Holy Spirit descend? At a moment when there was complete unity.

That same principle is at work today. When God's people are in agreement there is an atmosphere that invites healing, deliverance and victory. As the psalmist declared, "Behold, how good and how pleasant it is for brethren to dwell together in unity!" (Ps. 133:1, KJV).

God's Will to Heal

After my personal encounter with the Holy Spirit, I spent hundreds of hours in the Word. During this time I became convinced that miracles were not only possible, but it is God's *will* that His people be healed.

Many people declare, "He's the Savior of my soul," but fail to realize that the Lord is also the Savior of our physical bodies. Christ's death on the cross provided not only our salvation, but also our healing. First Peter 2:24 says, "He himself bore our sins in his body on the tree, so that we might die to sins and live for right-eousness; by his wounds you have been healed" (NIV).

It is His will that we be healed and remain healthy all the days of our lives. As God told Job, "You shall come to the grave at a full age, as a sheaf of grain ripens in its season" (Job 5:26, NKJV).

God promises that He will actually remove sickness from us. "And ye shall serve the Lord your God, and he shall bless thy bread and thy water; and I will take sickness away from the midst of thee" (Ex. 23:25, KJV).

I have often wondered why people — including born-again believers — have so little faith for their healing. More than once I have heard people accept their infirmities as inevitable, saying "Whatever will be, will be."

For many, the answer can be found in one word: *tradition*. They have always believed that way. We need to be reminded of what Jesus told the scribes and Pharisees when He said they were "making the word of God of no effect through your tradition which you have handed down" (Mark 7:13, NKJV).

Our customs and practices do not change God's Word. It is His will for us to live without sickness or disease. The writer of Proverbs states: "My son, give attention to my words...for they are life to those who find them, and health to all their flesh" (Prov. 4:20,22, NKJV).

A leper once knelt before Jesus and said, "If You are willing, You can make me clean" (Mark 1:40, NKJV). Christ put forth His hand, touched him and said, "I am willing; be cleansed" (v. 41).

Jesus said "I will," and His words are still true. If He was willing to heal only that one man, He would have said, "I will in your case." There would have been conditions.

Scripture clearly states that the Lord shows no partiality. The apostle Peter declared, "God is no respecter of persons" (Acts 10:34, KJV). Why is that important? It means that if He will heal one, He will heal another. And if He heals two, He will heal two million.

A Pair of Scissors

It continues to amaze me that some Christians believe that miracles ended with Christ's earthly ministry and that of the apostles.

Someone said to Oral Roberts, "I do not believe healing is for today."

Oral picked up a pair of scissors and said, "Give me your Bible."

He handed the Bible and the scissors back to the man and said, "I want you to cut out every scripture that deals with healing."

The gentleman responded, "I couldn't do that. I would be destroying the Word."

Oral Roberts paused for a moment and stated, "That is exactly what you do when you say that God does not heal."

Healing is not only for the past, but it is also for the present.

God told Moses, "If you diligently heed the voice of the Lord your God and do what is right in His sight, give ear to His commandments and keep all His statutes, I will put none of the diseases on you which I have brought on the Egyptians. For I am the Lord who heals you" (Ex. 15:26, NKJV).

God didn't tell Moses about what He did in the *past* for Abraham or Noah. God told Moses what He would do for him *today*. It was for *now*. If healing was for yesterday only, God would have said, "I was." But the ever-present God declared, "I am."

God is still God today. And since He is a *now* Lord, His promises are always *now* promises. The Bible is not a discourse of history, but a living Word for this very hour. It speaks in the present tense. "For all the promises of God in Him are Yes, and in Him Amen, to the glory of God through us" (2 Cor. 1:20, NKJV).

The Word of God is a present Word — it is always for today. When it was written it was *present*. Today it is *present*. It will always be *present*. Scripture declares that we are born again, "not of corruptible seed but incorruptible, through the word of God which lives and abides forever" (1 Pet. 1:23, NKJV).

When God Almighty declared, "I will make a new covenant," He did not mean that the teachings of the past should be dismissed. All Scripture — from Genesis to Revelation — is God inspired and is for today.

Jesus declares:

I am the resurrection and the life (John 11:25, NKJV).

> I am with you always, even unto the end of the world (Matt. 28:20, KJV).

> I am the way, the truth, and the life (John 14:6, KJV).

God says:

> For I am the Lord, I do not change (Mal. 3:6, NKJV).

> Jesus Christ is the same yesterday, today, and forever (Heb. 13:8, NKJV).

How do I respond when someone tells me, "The day of miracles is over"?

I tell them, "There is no such thing as a day of miracles. There is a God of miracles, and He does not change."

Remarkable Accounts

I am constantly amazed at the creativity of the God we serve. Many people are healed in our meetings before the service ever begins. Others are thousands of miles away when someone prays for them, and they are suddenly restored.

I cannot begin to explain how God heals, I only know that He does.

On the pages that follow, you will be inspired by the stories of:

- A nurse in Oklahoma who was tormented by a painful nerve disease

- A young boy in California who struggled with a rare blood disease

- A man in Indiana who was scheduled for heart bypass surgery

- A little girl in Texas with a congenital defect involving her eye

- A California restaurant manager whose malignant tumors appeared beyond hope

- A woman in Florida suffering from a tumor of her pituitary gland

- A Vermont woman with multiple orthopedic problems

- A young boy from Texas with a heart defect

- A New Mexico truck driver with an incapacitating back injury

- A young girl in Iowa who suffered an injury to her brain

As you read the remarkable accounts of people like Timmy Ballard, Julie Peel, Danny Garcia and Suzanne Frick, you will understand why I boldly proclaim the healing power of Christ.

Because of what I have experienced, what God has promised and what Christ has provided, I believe this is your day for a miracle!

3

"Now Is
the Time!"

J ANICE FUCHS WAS embarrassed.

On a cold winter's morning, January 10, 1994, she
was walking up to the building in Oklahoma City
where she was the vice president and director of clinical services of a hospice organization that cared for
terminally ill patients. Suddenly, her feet slipped on
the icy front steps of the building, and she fell onto
her arms which had extended in front of her as an
automatic reflex. "I was carrying some books and several files of paperwork I had taken home to work on,
and they went flying everywhere," Janice recalled.

She tried to get up but fell two more times, once

coming down on her right shoulder and another time coming down on her left wrist. People rushed over to help. "I could feel my face turning red. The whole scene must have looked like a slapstick comedy. I would get up, then fall, get up, then fall again," said the registered nurse, who was more concerned about the unwanted attention than about falling. Finally, gaining her composure, she gathered up her papers and went to work.

As the day progressed, pain continued to increase in her shoulder. "I tried to write, but my hand didn't want to cooperate," Janice remembered. "I had to dictate everything to my secretary."

Later that afternoon she thought, "I don't want to make a big thing out of this, but maybe I ought to be examined." After discussing it with her supervisor they called a mobile unit that came to her office and took an X-ray.

The radiologist reported she had a small fracture in her right elbow, so her right arm was put into a sling. "There wasn't much swelling, but it certainly did hurt," she recalled. At that time her left wrist indicated no pain or problems.

About two weeks later, as the pain continued in her right arm, her employer arranged for her to be assigned to an orthopedic doctor. Additional X-rays and an MRI (a test that provides images of soft tissues of the body) only indicated minor fractures; nothing serious. "My bones healed quickly, but every week my [right] arm hurt more than the week before," said Janice. The pain became so intense she had to quit working.

Beginning to Panic

Every day, Janice looked at her right hand and arm with increasing alarm. It was becoming larger and larger — and cold and blue. "I was beginning to panic," she said. "I felt surely somewhere there must be someone who could help me."

Her two grown sons, Michael and Gabor, lived nearby and tried to assist as much as possible, but they felt helpless. A friend who was also a registered nurse offered her assistance.

After several months of seeing the physicians, Janice was finally told, "We have nothing more we can offer you. Just try to keep your hand warm."

Taking matters into her own hands, in June 1994, Janice asked for a transfer from her assigned physician and made an appointment at a large, highly recommended orthopedic clinic. "They agreed to see me, but it was September 12 before they could schedule my first visit," she said. "By this time I had been to my family doctor and to the emergency room at the hospital on several nights with excruciating pain. There were times I thought I was going to die and hoped I would."

In July, Janice had another injury — this time to her left wrist. She was trying to stand up from a seated position and pushed off with her left hand (since her right hand was too painful to use). She hyperextended her wrist and experienced immediate pain. In a short while her left arm began showing the same symptoms as the right arm — swelling, numbness, pain and coldness.

Janice consulted several physicians, but no one

knew what to do for her. All they could tell her was that parts of the circulatory and nervous systems in her arms were completely shut down, but they didn't know why.

Janice was counting the days until her first appointment with her new doctor. She had already learned he was one of the finest orthopedic specialists in the region. "By that September day my hands were badly swollen," she remembered clearly.

Finally, an Answer

The clinic nurse put a gown on Janice and told her to sit on the examination table. When the doctor walked into the room he looked at his new patient and exclaimed, "Oh, my goodness!" Then, quickly looking down at her chart to catch her name, he said, "Janice, you have severe reflex sympathetic dystrophy."

After further examination, her new doctor continued, "We've got to schedule you for a sympathetic ganglion block" — a procedure where they use a needle to go into the nerves in the spinal area and place medication there to numb the nerves. The specialist explained to Janice, "Our goal is to block the signals coming out of that particular center of nerves." He immediately arranged for Janice to begin physical therapy.

Three days later doctors performed the first of three sympathetic blocks on Janice for the pain in her right arm and hand. Finally, after eight months of unrelenting pain, Janice began to feel some relief from her agony. The treatments worked, and the reflex sympathetic dystrophy (RSD) in her right arm and hand showed some improvement.

The more serious problem, however, was in Janice's left wrist. The RSD in her left arm did not respond to the sympathetic blocks as the right arm had.

Janice went through a more intensive series of the sympathetic blocks (a total of eight more). Each time she hoped for relief but found none. To add to this problem, she began experiencing pain in her right shoulder which doctors attempted to treat with physical therapy.

Graduation Day

To learn more about her RSD and its treatment, Janice was asked to attend an eight-week intensive educational program at the rehabilitation center where she was receiving her physical therapy. It was directed by a physician who was a leading authority on the disease. Patients with the illness came from several states.

She remembered the first day she attended. "They were having a session, and the social worker in charge said, 'Today, there are four people who are graduating, and I'd like each of you to tell what you have learned about the disease, what you can do for yourselves and what you think the rest of your life is going to be like.'"

Janice listened intently as each patient said essentially the same thing: They had all completed the program, yet not one had been cured of RSD. They said, "You're going to hurt, and doctors can give you treatment, but you'll become progressively worse."

WORKER'S COMPENSATION PROGRESS REPORT

WORKER'S COMP CARRIER	NAME		EMPL'S	
	ADDRESS		EMP	Janice F. Morse
			DATE OF SP	01-10-94
			CLAIM #	

DATE	DESCRIPTION OF SERVICE	CHARGE
03-14-95	STATEMENT ATTACHED	

PROGRESS REPORT

This is an orthopedic report on the above patient. Ms. Morse returns for follow up examination today on her right shoulder. She apparently has been attending physical therapy at Priority Care in regards to her right shoulder and been receiving modalities as well as exercise treatments. She reports to me that her shoulder is still sore and tender principally it hurts her in the front or anterior aspect of the shoulder and also back into the parascapular area and posterior aspect of the shoulder as well. Any type of forced abduction or external rotation is quite painful for her. She has not had a recurrence of reflex sympathetic dystrophy of her right arm or shoulder area.

Physical examination today reveals that range of motion of her right shoulder is limited. She can abduct about 90°, externally rotate about 60° before there is pain, and before she voluntarily limits motion. I notice that she had extreme signs and symptoms of reflex sympathetic dystrophy on her left upper extremity. I don't notice the same on the right. So, her skin is of fairly normal appearance, color, sensation is intact, and there is no obvious hypersensitivity like there is on the left side.

This patient is still complaining of right shoulder pain and I think it is reasonable to continue a course of physical therapy in regards to the right shoulder. I certainly do not think that this patient is a candidate for any type of surgical intervention in regards to her shoulder. Conservative treatment is indicated in her condition. She informs me that she is being considered for a dorsal column stimulator to combat the rather severe reflex sympathetic dystrophy of her left arm, and judging by her physical examination today and just the appearance of her left arm, I would go ahead and encourage placement of a dorsal column stimulator by ████.

This patient will return to see me in six weeks. At that time we may consider using Dexamethasone patch to treat her shoulder condition.

I declare, under penalty of perjury, that I have examined this report and all the statements contained herein and, to the best of my knowledge and belief, they are true, correct, and complete

03-14-95

This report describes the range of motion limitations of Janice's right shoulder and the "rather severe reflex sympathetic dystrophy of her left arm."

When Janice saw that some of the graduates were leaving in wheelchairs, she said out loud, "Maybe you are signing up for that program, but I'm not."

She also learned that a percentage of those with RSD attempt suicide.

By November she found herself totally consumed with treatment for her disease. She was seeing her orthopedic specialist, having meetings with the doctor who was working with her on the sympathetic blocks, and went to physical therapy five days a week.

The months rolled by, and Janice didn't stray from the path her new doctors had prescribed. All they could tell her was, "It looks like this will take a long time."

On March 30, 1995, Janice underwent surgery. This was to install a dorsal column stimulator on a trial basis to see if it eased her pain. "Essentially," she explained, "they put electrodes in your spinal column."

Since she tolerated the device well, the doctors surgically implanted the stimulator permanently on April 25, 1995. "I had wires down my back, and the battery-operated, computer-controlled generator was in my buttocks," said Janice. "I was willing to accept anything to ease the anguish."

Much of the time during her ordeal with the disease, Janice required a nurse's aide. After the surgery, she required the aide full-time to help her with even the simplest of tasks. More and more she stayed in bed and took pain pills that never seemed to be strong enough. Her left arm and hand were still swollen and blue. Janice recalled, "My hand was cold and clammy."

The pain in her right shoulder also continued, and the range of motion in her shoulder was limited. She could only raise her right arm a short distance until it was too painful to go any further.

On Friday, May 5, she was released from physical therapy. "There's nothing more we can do for you," she was told.

Turning the Dial

Janice had known for several months that hope of relief from her condition was remote. At that point she turned to God's Word for help. Using a concordance, she looked up every scripture in the Bible with the words *heal, healed, healing* and *healer.* She read each verse and began to believe God could miraculously touch her.

One day she accidentally turned the television dial to a channel that was carrying our program, *This Is Your Day!* "Isn't that interesting!" she thought to herself as she saw people giving testimony to God's healing power.

Across the bottom of the TV screen was the announcement that our entire crusade team would be coming to the Myriad Convention Center in downtown Oklahoma City on May 11 and 12, 1995. When Janice told June, a close acquaintance, about the upcoming meetings, her friend said, "I think we should go."

"I can't even walk more than a few feet," Janice sadly responded. She was having pain in her left leg, and was afraid that the RSD was beginning to affect it as well.

"I know it will be difficult," answered her friend, "but they have a new wheelchair at the Presbyterian church, and we'll borrow it."

Janice told her, "Well, I'm not going unless I'm sure I'm going to be healed."

"That's between you and God. I'm just the driver," replied June.

Just before leaving for the service, Janice Fuchs turned off the dorsal column stimulator (only sixteen days after it was implanted) and removed all of the pain medication from her purse. "What am I going to need these for?" she said to herself in an act of faith.

It took two people to help Janice into the wheelchair. They drove to the convention center several hours before the opening service on Thursday, arriving so early they were near the front of the line. The waiting was painful, but that is how it had been for the past sixteen months.

When the doors opened, she was guided down the ramp by her friend to a special area reserved for those in wheelchairs.

From the moment the choir started rehearsing, Janice was singing right along. "I grew up in a Baptist church and most of those songs were very familiar," she recounted.

Janice stated that when the service began, "I got so happy while I was singing that I raised both of my arms up into the air." She had forgotten all about her doctor's orders not to move her elbows away from her body due to a large, unhealed incision from her neck to her tailbone because of the recent generator implant.

"The moment my hands were raised I felt

something happening up and down the incision on my back," she vividly recalled. Every bit of pain stopped immediately. She turned to her friend and exclaimed, "June, my incision just healed!"

No one laid hands on her and prayed for her at that moment. It just happened.

As the singing continued, Janice again lifted her hands to praise the Lord in the atmosphere filled with the Spirit's anointing.

Janice describes what transpired next. "All of a sudden it felt just as though I had stepped into a whirlpool of hot water. It started around my feet, then came up my ankles and around my legs. It continued up my body, over my head and surged to my upraised hands." She said to herself, "Mercy sakes, what's going on here?"

As the whirlpool sensation subsided she looked down at her hand because it had stopped hurting. "It was suddenly absolutely normal, as perfect as it had ever been in my life," she said. "The swelling was totally gone. The blueness had disappeared."

Janice was so excited that she leaped out of her wheelchair and ran down the aisle toward the platform. Janice said, "Two wonderful little ushers grabbed my arms and said, 'Lady, where are you going?' I responded, 'I don't know, but I've got to tell somebody I'm healed!'"

They told her, "It's not time yet."

When the ushers learned she had come forward without her wheelchair, one held onto her while the other went back and found June. They were moved to seats closer to the platform.

I, Lala ███████████ R.N. had under my care, for three months, Janice Szekely Fuchs. I made visits to her home and directed care given to her by a nursing assistant, ███████████.

Following Janice's surgery & hospitalization the last week of april 1995, I took her to my home where, with the help of ms. Vinson we could give her 24 hr Nursing care. She remained in my home under my care until May 12, 1995 Her doctor's verbal instructions to me included, bed rest with Bath room priviledges for the first week. The second week Janice was able to walk to the dining room for meals & even step out into the sun in the back yard.

███████████████

This is a note from the nurse who cared for Janice after the surgery to install the dorsal column stimulator. Notice that care was discontinued one day after she was touched by God at the crusade.

Later in the service, I asked if anyone had a testimony of God's healing. The two ushers ran over to Janice. "Now is the time!" they told her.

She came to the platform and publicly praised the Lord that her hand had returned to its normal size and the pain was totally gone.

What Happened?

That night she slept like a baby. No more medication. No more suffering. No need for assistance.

Janice couldn't wait for her next doctor's appointment on June 13. "I didn't say a word," she recalled. "I just waited at the end of the examination table and held out my hands."

The physician took one look and exclaimed, "What happened?"

"I've been healed. It's a miracle of God!" she joyously reported.

After staring at her for a moment, he said, "Janice, I believe in prayer. I really do." Then he added, "I guess I can discharge you. You don't need me anymore."

Returning to the rehabilitation center was another memorable moment for Janice. People were astonished to see her walk in with hands and arms that were perfectly normal.

Those at the center who had worked with her for so long called in therapists, secretaries and other medical professionals to see what had happened to Janice.

They were dumfounded by the sudden change in her condition.

June 13, 1995 — *post Healing* 5/11/95

Re: Janice Morse

████ ██ ████:

Ms. Morse came to see me today. She finished her extensive RSD Program at the Occupational Health Center. She had a trial of dorsal column stimulator and a permanent one placed and is doing fantastic. The only problem she has is a few weeks ago she fell down the stairs at her home and bruised her back but she did not injure the dorsal column pack and she states her back is all right now and she feels better. She stated that most of her symptoms of RSD are under control and she is doing remarkably well. She is not taking much medication and she is feeling better. She is acting and feeling like a different person.

Physical Examination: My examination today revealed remarkable resolution of most of her RSD symptoms, remarkable improvement with range of motion, no more stiffness, and good use of her extremity. She looks remarkably better.

Recommendation: I am recommending that we do a vocational assessment on this lady and then see her back in one month and at that time I will do final rating and release. In the meantime she is to continue her same program. If you have any questions please do not hesitate to call me.

I declare under penalty of perjury that I have examined this report and all statements contained herein, and to the best of my knowledge and belief, they are true, correct, and complete.

Sincerely,

This note from Janice's doctor shows that she no longer suffered from the symptoms of reflex sympathetic dystrophy. It is dated June 13, 1995, just one month after she attended the crusade.

Janice had not turned the dorsal column stimulator back on since the day of her healing on May 11, 1995, and she no longer took pain medication. The next time she went to see her doctor, Janice asked that the dorsal column stimulator be removed. The battery pack to the stimulator was causing her pain in the area where it was implanted.

"I don't need this thing anymore," she happily told the physician who had it implanted.

Her request to remove the stimulator posed a rather delicate problem. "That's a twenty-thousand-dollar apparatus you have in you," she was told. "And you just want me to go in there and take it out?" He added, "Your insurance company is going to be livid. They will think I ordered an unnecessary operation." He suggested revising the stimulator and reimplanting it in a different place.

Janice said, "Tell them I needed it then. I just don't need it now!"

Finally, on October 31, 1995, the generator was removed.

Janice may have been embarrassed the morning she slipped on the icy pavement, but today she has no reservations proclaiming that the Lord has healed her completely.

Lessons From the Great Physician

Back in the boat, Jesus and the disciples recrossed the sea to Jesus' hometown. They were hardly out of the boat when some men carried a paraplegic on a stretcher and set him down in front of them. Jesus, impressed by their bold belief, said to the paraplegic, "Cheer up, son. I forgive your sins." Some religion scholars whispered, "Why that's blasphemy!"

Jesus knew what they were thinking, and said, "Why this gossipy whispering? Which do you think is simpler: to say, 'I forgive your sins,' or, 'Get up and walk'? Well, just so it's clear that I'm the Son of Man and authorized to do either, or both..." At this he turned to the paraplegic and said, "Get up. Take your bed and go home." And the man did it. The crowd was awestruck, amazed and pleased that God had authorized Jesus to work among them this way.

Matthew 9:1-8

The crowd was awestruck, amazed and pleased that God had authorized Jesus to work among them this way.

4

A Good Friday
for Timmy

IT'S PROBABLY HEREDITARY," thought Teri Ballard
in 1991 when her nine-year-old son, Timmy, began
complaining of migraine headaches. She had often suffered with migraines, so she tried not to worry too
much.

During the months that followed, Teri and her husband, Tim Sr., became alarmed by the sudden
deterioration in the health of their handsome son.
"Timmy would come down the stairs to go to school,
and he would begin to have pain in his legs," recalled
his mother.

The pain was first attributed to growing pains, but

the Ballards would soon discover that it was a much more serious problem.

Tim Sr. and Teri were married in 1981, committing their future and their home in Brea, California, to the Lord. Their first son, Timmy, was born the following year. He weighed only four pounds and ten ounces. Later arrived Aaron, who would be a brother and a needed friend to Timmy during the unexpected times ahead.

The Ballards were deeply involved in their Catholic church and in an outreach ministry, Breath of the Spirit International. They poured their lives into their children and were sensitive, loving parents.

As each day passed, the full magnitude of Timmy's illness became clearer. "At one point he began losing weight, about a pound a day. He quickly deteriorated, going from seventy-three pounds down to sixty-one. I could carry him in my arms," said Teri.

Once when his mother looked at his face and noticed what appeared to be a huge bruise on his chin, she started to panic. "The moment I saw it, I knew this was not a normal bruise — not like he had bumped into something," recalled Teri.

Timmy's mother began to check out his body. "That day there were huge bruises everywhere, on his back, on his legs and on his arms. There had to be something seriously wrong," she remembered.

Dashed Hopes

Timmy was finally admitted to the hospital on February 2, 1992. Doctors were puzzled when they discovered bone age results showing nine-year-old Timmy had the bones of a seven-year-old. They began doing further tests in hopes of finding out what was wrong with him. A CT scan, an EEG (which records brain activity) and an MRI were part of Timmy's routine as the physicians worked diligently to identify this mysterious intruder that had taken up residence in his now-frail body.

"It took the doctors six months to diagnose him fully," stated his mother. "At first they thought he had leukemia. Then they spoke of the possibility of a brain tumor or even bone cancer."

Finally, the day arrived when the Ballards were told, "Your son has a very rare blood disease." Timmy was diagnosed with anti-phospholipid syndrome, which deteriorates the blood cells, weakens the body and can be life-threatening. Basically, Timmy's immune system was producing antibodies that it should not have been, and these antibodies were attacking tissue throughout his body.

The parents were told that only eight other cases like Timmy's had been reported in California. It also became apparent that some tiny areas of abnormality on the MRI scan of his brain probably represented small infarctions or strokes caused by this disease.

Unfortunately, the doctors had found the problem but not the cure. "The hopes we had for Timmy appeared to be dashed," said his father. "It seemed his life was painfully unraveling before our eyes."

By this time Timmy was unable to attend school and was being tutored at home. Tremors developed in his hands which made it difficult for him to do many things children take for granted. After playing

BALLARD, TIMOTHY

Admitted   2/5/92
Discharged 2/7/92

DISCHARGE SUMMARY

ADMITTING DIAGNOSES:
1. Weight loss of thirteen pounds.
2. Severe headache.
3. Severe leg pain.

FINAL DIAGNOSES:
1. Weight loss of thirteen pounds.
2. Severe headache.
3. Severe leg pain.

HISTORY OF PRESENT ILLNESS:
Timothy is a nine-year-old with an eight-week history of weight loss, most severe over the last two weeks. He evidently had had a poor appetite, however it has picked up recently. The weight loss has been complicated by severe leg pain. Usually the leg pain involves the muscles of the thighs and calves. Initially this was thought to be growing pain, however it has become much more severe, especially over the last week. The pain is severe over the right leg just above the patella and, at times, his leg has given out on him.

Mother notes that he has not looked well and that especially when he is in pain his face becomes pale and dull. The pain lasts about two to six hours. He does not actually have morning stiffness but the leg begins to hurt after going down the stairs. He has not had any trauma or fall in this area.

He has been having headaches, which started about nine months ago after a fall from the bed. Usually the headaches are on the right side and he describes them as being a "dull knife sticking into" his "brain." Advil helps somewhat. He denies any photophobia or aura. He feels nauseated and on a few occasions he has vomited. The headaches usually come after activity.

He has not had any fevers. He did have the flu in December. He has not had any polyuria or polydipsia. There has been no rash except under his axilla which mother feels is secondary to sweating. He has had asthma since he was 11 months of age but has not required any medications recently. He had travel history to Israel and Rome. His stools have been softer and in the past there have been no ova or parasite noted in his stool. Review of systems is otherwise negative.

DISCHARGE SUMMARY   Page 1

After a full review of Timmy's systems, doctors could not find the cause of Timmy's illnesses. Consequently Timmy spent two days in the hospital and was discharged with the same diagnoses he received upon admission.

for only ten or fifteen minutes, his strength would be totally drained.

Fortunately, he was a fighter and refused to give up. Timmy remembered, "I was on medication every day just to keep me going. There were times I wondered if I was going to make it, but somehow I just knew one day I was going to get better. I would say, 'Hey, God is with us!'"

The disease continued its unrelenting attack. "One EEG brain scan revealed unusual activity in the periotal lobes of the brain," said Teri. The outlook was not good.

Fighting a Battle

The only anchor the Ballards could grasp was their unswerving faith in the healing power of Christ. "We knew we were not walking through this alone," she stated.

One night, before Timmy went to bed, she felt led of the Lord to tell her son, "I promise you — and Momma's going to prophesy to you — that every bruise on your body will turn into glory." She felt he had been counted worthy to be acquainted with the sufferings of Christ.

Their faith, however, continued to be put to the test. The following year was painful. Each member of the family fought his or her own private battle. Timmy's brother Aaron wondered, "Am I losing my closest friend?" He prayed, "Lord, is Timmy ever going to be healed and play with me again?"

Tim Sr. said, "There were days we felt we were about to lose him. We knew we were fighting a spiritual battle that was being manifested in the physical. We would literally bind the forces of satan against attack." He added, "I had many, many questions. I remember asking the Lord, 'What is Your purpose in this?' Then, at other times, I was pleading with God not to take him."

The whole family knew the Lord could heal Timmy. A newspaper account of his illness recognized the faith that each of the Ballards had in God's power.

I often saw the Ballards when we conducted crusades in Southern California — volunteering their services to help in any way they could.

In the Anaheim Miracle Crusade, December 10, 1993, the family came to the platform, and I asked thousands attending that night to unite their hearts as Timmy, then eleven years old, simply asked God once again to heal his body.

I stood with Timmy and his parents as I told the audience, "These are some of the most precious people on earth. The devil is trying to take Timmy's life, but we are not going to allow it."

In a tender moment that was being televised, Timmy quietly spoke these words: "Please heal me, Lord. I've been asking You too long. Please Lord, just heal me right now."

I prayed, "We all agree with him, Lord. We all agree with him that little Timmy is going to be healed — that this evil disease in his body is going to die." Then I looked up to the Lord and said, "Oh, God, if I could give it to him I would, but I can't, Lord. I'm a man. But You are the healer. You are the Great Physician. You are no respecter of persons. You heal this boy. Heal Timmy, in Jesus' name."

At that moment Timmy fell under the power of God. As he lay on the floor, he heard the voice of the Lord say something specifically to him.

I told the crusade audience, "I wish you could see his face, crying there."

"Timmy, you know He loves you," I quietly whispered to him.

Then Timmy told me the words the Lord had just said to him, and I shared them with the audience. "The Lord just spoke to him on the floor. He said, 'It's not time yet, but it's coming soon, Timmy. It's coming soon!'"

"I Can't Tell You"

Three months later, the week before Easter 1994, Teri took her two sons to a Catholic mass. Timmy was prayed for and once again he felt God's holy presence. For the second time, the Lord spoke to Timmy. This time he heard specific instructions about what was to take place.

Timmy remembered, "God said 'On Friday you are going to be healed.' And I believed that with all of my heart."

Teri said, "He came to where Aaron and I were sitting with big tears in his eyes." He scooted up next to his brother, put his arms around him and said, "Aaron, Jesus talked to me, but I can't tell you what He said."

His mother heard those words and asked, "What happened?" but Timmy wouldn't say. On the way home she asked again, and he replied, "I can't tell you. The Lord told me I can't tell anyone until He says I can."

The next week was the most difficult one of

Timmy's life. He was extremely ill and in great pain.

The following Friday, April 1, 1994, was Good Friday. Thousands of people gathered with us at the Arrowhead Pond Arena in Anaheim, California, for a special communion service in remembrance of the death of Jesus Christ, who willingly suffered that we may know life.

As the choir sang "Alleluia," I said, "People, the healing power of the Holy Ghost is here." I responded to the direction of the Lord to name specific infirmities that were being healed.

Timmy remembered that moment, too. "I was hit by the power of God so strong that it almost knocked me off my feet," he recalled. "It happened very quickly. My brother was sitting next to me, and my parents were helping the ministry team."

At that point in the service I asked, "Every person that feels or felt God's power come on you, and you know that God has touched you and healed you — or is healing you now — get up quickly out of your seat, and line up to my left and to my right."

When Timmy heard those words, he turned to his brother and said, "I've got to go!"

Aaron asked, "What for?"

Timmy replied, "I've just got to go."

Tim Sr. remembered, "We were working with people who had come forward, asking them to share their testimony. The lines were very long, and suddenly I saw Timmy at the end of one of the lines. I thought, 'What is he doing? He just can't get up on the platform and say he is healed without proof.'"

As Teri was working with the ministry team, she

also saw Timmy coming toward the platform. She walked back to talk to him, and he told her, "It's time! I've got to go tell Pastor.' "

Timmy later told me, "Pastor Benny, I don't know what made you turn around as I approached the platform, but you did. You just looked at me and knew — you just knew!"

When Timmy came up to the stage, I asked the audience, "Do you remember him? Do you remember this little boy?"

The entire arena burst into applause. Many of them recalled the night in December when this precious young man was on the platform.

"His day has come!" I shouted. "His day has come!"

God had ordained something far beyond what the Ballards could plan or imagine.

"Timmy, what is happening?" I asked him.

He replied, "The Lord said, 'You are going to be healed on Friday.' And He said, 'Don't tell anyone until it happens.'" Then Timmy looked at me and said, "It's time!"

Tears of joy fell down the faces of many that Good Friday evening. Our hearts were filled with gratitude for what the Lord was doing in Timmy's life.

"Wake Up! Wake Up!"

By Easter morning, just two days later, the changes in Timmy began to present clear evidence that he had received a supernatural touch from God. His mother said, "One of the first signs was in the fourteen warts that had earlier formed on his body. They all fell off that Good Friday."

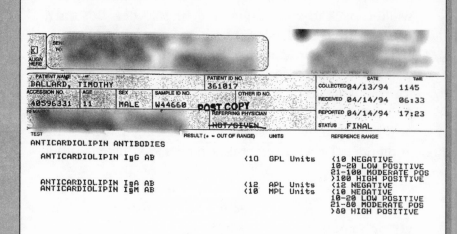

PATIENT NAME				PATIENT ID NO.		DATE	TIME
BALLARD, TIMOTHY				361017		COLLECTED 04/13/94	1145
ACCESSION NO.	AGE	SEX	SAMPLE ID NO.	OTHER ID NO.		RECEIVED 04/14/94	06:33
40596331	11	MALE	W44660	POST COPY		REPORTED 04/14/94	17:23
REMARKS				REFERRING PHYSICIAN			
				NOT GIVEN		STATUS FINAL	

TEST	RESULT (* = OUT OF RANGE)	UNITS	REFERENCE RANGE
ANTICARDIOLIPIN ANTIBODIES			
ANTICARDIOLIPIN IgG AB	<10	GPL Units	<10 NEGATIVE
			10-20 LOW POSITIVE
			21-100 MODERATE POS
			>100 HIGH POSITIVE
ANTICARDIOLIPIN IgA AB	<12	APL Units	<12 NEGATIVE
ANTICARDIOLIPIN IgM AB	<10	MPL Units	<10 NEGATIVE
			10-20 LOW POSITIVE
			21-80 MODERATE POS
			>80 HIGH POSITIVE

This blood test result, given just two weeks after Timmy's
healing, shows negative for anticardiolipin antibodies,
which had been elevated on previous tests.

That week Timmy's appetite suddenly returned. Within the next few days he was again playing with his brother. His energy increased dramatically.

Timmy was given another blood test, this time the outlook was different.

Early one morning while the family slept, the phone rang. It was Timmy's doctor with the good news that the tests showed no antibodies.

Teri ran into Timmy's room and exclaimed, "Wake up! Wake up! Momma has the most beautiful news. The antibodies are gone!"

He looked at his mother and replied matter-of-factly, "I know."

"Oh, did Daddy tell you?" Teri asked.

Timmy looked up and said, "No. Jesus told me." And he went back to sleep.

The Ballards had walked through the valley of the shadow of death, but the Lord was always there. For Timmy and his family, Good Friday will always be a day of special celebration.

Lessons From
the Great Physician

As Jesus entered the village of Capernaum, a Roman captain came up in a panic and said, "Master, my servant is sick. He can't walk. He's in terrible pain."

Jesus said, "I'll come and heal him."

"Oh, no," said the captain. "I don't want to put you to all that trouble. Just give the order and my servant will be fine. I'm a man who takes orders and gives orders. I tell one soldier, 'Go,' and he goes; to another, 'Come,' and he comes; to my slave, 'Do this,' and he does it."

Taken aback, Jesus said, "I've yet to come across this kind of simple trust in Israel, the very people who are supposed to know all about God and how he works. This man is the vanguard of many outsiders who will soon be coming from all directions — streaming in from the east, pouring in from the west, sitting down at God's kingdom banquet table alongside Abraham, Isaac, and Jacob. Then those who grew up 'in the faith' but had no faith will find themselves out in the cold, outsiders to grace and wondering what happened."

Matthew 8:5-12

**Taken aback, Jesus said,
"I've yet to come across this kind
of simple trust in Israel..."**

5

New Steps
to Climb

I T WAS ABOUT 11:30 P.M. on March 2, 1991. Forty-
five-year-old Jerry Wood and his wife, Kathy, were
relaxing, watching television in the bedroom of their
home in Evansville, Indiana. Suddenly, without warn-
ing, Jerry had a serious heart attack.

"I was scared beyond belief," said Jerry, the manager of a gasoline terminal on the Ohio River just
south of Evansville. "Sharp pains shot down both of
my arms to my wrists, and I fell to the floor."

Kathy hurriedly dialed 911. "Quick. Send an ambulance," she said. "My husband is dying."

Jerry doesn't remember much of what took place

when the emergency medics arrived. "I could feel people putting things in my mouth and sticking me with needles, but I could not hear or see anyone," he recalled. "I just knew I was dying."

Jerry blacked out again and again. As the ambulance raced to the hospital, the medics placed nitroglycerin under his tongue and injected morphine into his arm.

From the first moment of the attack, Jerry pleaded, "Please, God, don't let me die. I'm not ready! I'm not ready!"

Hitting Rock Bottom

Talking to God was not a regular part of Jerry's life. When he returned from Vietnam, he was an angry young man. "I came home hating the world and hating myself," he confessed. "My life consisted of heavy drinking, fighting, lying, cheating and somehow hurting everyone who came into my path." To bolster his macho image he toted a gun and became increasingly dependent on drugs.

After a failed marriage and the death of both of his parents, Jerry hit rock bottom.

"Finally, in 1984, when I was lonely and desperately trying to get my life straightened out, Kathy came into my life. She was strong-willed and exactly what I needed," he said.

Jerry and Kathy joined a church, but God was not the focus of their lives. "We rarely attended a service," he admitted. "My life centered around my work, my motorcycle, our boat and a new pickup truck. Sunday was the only day I could play with my toys. I was far too busy for God."

Now, confined to a hospital bed, Jerry had to face some new realities. The cardiologist had performed angioplasty by inserting a tiny balloon into the blocked coronary artery to widen it. The doctors explained, "Your heart is permanently damaged, and you have tissue and artery damage you will never get over." They also told him that he would have to greatly reduce his work schedule, rest two hours each afternoon, avoid lifting heavy objects and begin a strict, special diet.

Change did not come easily. Nine months later, while Jerry and Kathy were shopping at a local department store, he was stunned by a bout of severe chest pain caused by unstable angina, a condition that can cause the same intense pain as a heart attack. "I landed on the floor under a rack of clothing and was again rushed to the hospital," he remembered. Another catheterization was performed, and his doctors decided to treat his blockage with medication.

Part of Jerry's work at the gasoline terminal was to climb to the top of large storage tanks to check the fuel gauges. "There are 102 steps to the top," he explained. "I know. I've counted them many, many times."

Now he was taking ten pills a day and wearing nitroglycerin patches under each arm to enable him to work. "There were times when I had to stop halfway up my climb and take nitro tablets before I could continue," he recalled. "Often I laid down when I reached the top of the tank so I wouldn't pass out."

On November 20, 1992, the night before the wedding

61

of his oldest son, Jerry was helping to prepare the reception hall when he again started having severe pains in his arms. Not wanting to spoil a happy occasion, he didn't tell anyone. "The next day I made it through the ceremony. After the reception I went to our home to get a vacuum cleaner to help tidy the building," he recounted. "As I was coming down the front steps, I started blacking out. I tried to make it to the car but fell on the pavement."

A neighbor contacted his wife, and Jerry was hospitalized a third time. "During my recovery it finally dawned on me that if it were not for the grace of God I would have been dead long before." That's when the Woods found a Bible-believing church and began attending regularly.

After the fourth visit to the hospital for chest pains, Jerry's doctor told him that he should consider applying for disability because his physical condition would not allow him to do his current job. "I felt so worthless. I couldn't mow the grass, carry in firewood or even wash the car," he stated. "I was limited in the distance I could walk and could not go shopping. With the slightest exertion, I quickly ran out of breath and experienced chest pains."

Kathy became the breadwinner in the family.

The Coach to Cincinnati

Early in 1993 someone told Jerry and Kathy that our crusade team was coming to Cincinnati, Ohio. "I had seen your show on television several times and immediately wanted to go," said Jerry.

When Jerry mentioned the crusade to some friends at his church, so many people wanted to attend that he reserved a bus from a charter coach company for which he had done some part-time driving. They made space available on the bus for other people in their town to go also.

The services were scheduled on March 25 and 26, 1993.

Just days before the planned trip to Cincinnati, Jerry was hospitalized a fifth time. The doctors informed him, "We have done four heart catheterizations and four angioplasties. If you continue to have problems, we need to make arrangements for you to have heart bypass surgery."

"Oh, no!" exclaimed Jerry. "I can't do that now. I have a trip to make that is very important."

"If you don't have surgery immediately, it is hard to tell what might happen," they warned him.

"No, I just have to wait," insisted Jerry. "But as soon as I get back from Ohio I'll be ready." The doctors just shook their heads.

On March 23, Jerry checked himself out of the hospital. The next day the busload of people left for Cincinnati — with Jerry driving the bus.

The trip to Cincinnati was almost a disaster. "The bus failed to start and had to be repaired," Jerry recalled. "It was raining. The temperature controls didn't work, and the passengers were obviously worried about the health of the driver!"

The group from Evansville reached Cincinnati in time for the morning service. Jerry stated, "I will never forget, Pastor Benny, when you stopped in the middle of your message to say, 'If there is anyone here that is not absolutely sure you would go to be with the Lord if you were to die this very moment, I want you to walk down to this altar right now.'"

When Jerry and Kathy heard those words they rushed to the front of the auditorium. Jerry said, "It was at that moment I surrendered my life totally to Christ. I asked Him to be the Lord of my life and to live within my heart forever."

That evening when Jerry drove the chartered bus back to the arena, the parking lots were jammed. "After letting our group off at the entrance, I finally found a place to park at the back of the facility," Jerry recalled. His family and several friends stayed with him because of their fears for his condition. "There was only one problem. I had to climb at least sixty steps to reach the doors to the arena. I began having chest pains almost immediately and had to stop and take my nitro tablets."

"Jerry was in terrible pain, and we were all concerned for his condition," said Marian LaChance, one of their friends who had stayed with them. They finally made it inside the arena.

Jerry said, "We lost our group in the crowd, and were told by the ushers that the only seats available were at the very top of the arena. It looked like an impossible climb." He struggled with each step, and by the time they reached the top, Kathy was in tears.

"I was so afraid he was going to have another heart attack and die. He was getting worse and worse," said Kathy.

A Burst of Wind

The service that night was powerful. Halfway through the meeting the Lord told me He was going to do something very special. "There are many people the Lord wants to heal right now," I announced. "Please remain still because a healing wind is about to come through this building."

Jerry and Kathy were standing — holding hands and praying for their son Jeremy. About that time a burst of air hit Jerry in the face, and he fell to the floor between the row of seats. Jerry commented later, "This was all new to me. I had never been slain by the power of God. I had seen other people fall under the Lord's power, yet I didn't understand it."

At that moment a woman who had come on the bus with Jerry but was not part of his church group came running over from another section to tell Jerry, "You just received your new heart. You are healed!"

Kathy also remembers that moment. "When I bent down to touch him, his skin was hot, and his clothes were wringing with sweat — as if he had been in a shower," she said.

When Jerry first attempted to stand he remembered, "My legs were so wobbly I didn't know if I was going to make it. But within a few seconds I knew something awesome had happened. Suddenly my entire body felt different. I knew that I had been healed. It seemed that a huge load was lifted from my body. I felt as though I could run for a mile."

Jerry did not come to the platform to give his testimony that night, but he didn't hesitate to proclaim

God's goodness. "After we returned to the motel, I ran up and down the halls telling everyone the wonderful news. Some people looked at us as if we had lost our minds, but I didn't care. I threw away my nitro tablets, and we sang and praised the Lord all night!"

Searching for Proof

Jerry could hardly wait to go back to the gasoline terminal on Monday morning to tell people what the Lord had done. "About seventy-five to one hundred trucks a day pass through the facility, and all of those drivers knew how sick I had been."

"The first thing I did was to rush out to the biggest gasoline tank and run up the steps — two at a time — praising God all the way!" he exclaimed. "When I raced back down they all gathered around me, thinking I was going to have another attack. But I told them not to worry. I was totally healed."

Jerry, wanting medical proof of his healing, went to his doctor and asked that a thallium stress test be scheduled.

Jerry had been given thallium stress tests on a regular basis prior to the crusade. Each time he was put on a treadmill and monitored to see how close he could come to his target heart rate. When his heart was beating as fast as possible, doctors injected him with thallium and exercised him for another minute or so. The thallium would allow doctors to better look at Jerry's heart and would help reveal any abnormalities.

However Jerry got a disappointing response from his doctor. "I was astonished when my physician said a thallium stress test wasn't necessary and that I should continue my medication. He also emphasized the urgency of a bypass operation," said Jerry.

Determined to be re-tested, Jerry asked a physician who attended their church to arrange for him to see another heart specialist for tests.

"When I arrived at the clinic, I did not tell them about my past condition because I wanted an unbiased report," he said. "I also avoided answering some of the questions I was supposed to fill out before the exam."

The goal had always been for Jerry to reach his target heart rate, which was 85-90 percent of the

Jerry Wood
Thallium Stress Test Results

Date Test Given	Target Heart Rate*	Top Heart Rate Achieved	% Target Heart Rate Achieved	Impression
3/13/91	158	126	79%	Abnormal
1/24/92	157	118	75%	Abnormal
3/18/92	157	113	72%	Abnormal
8/17/92	157	119	76%	Abnormal
3/23/93	156	108	69%	Abnormal
Jerry healed at Benny Hinn crusade March 26, 1993				
4/16/93	156	156	100%	NORMAL
1/18/94	155	167	100+%	Normal
* adjusted by age				

maximum rate doctors predicted his heart could beat, based on his age. This was attempted by having Jerry walk on a treadmill. He had never been able to reach that goal.

In 1991, not long after his heart attack, they had to stop the test after he had only reached 79 percent of his target heart rate because he started having shortness of breath. The results of each test thereafter fluctuated in the 70 percentile range. "I would have chest pains and have to stop," recalled Jerry.

This time the test was different for Jerry. Nine minutes into the test, the technician asked him to stop.

"Why?" asked Jerry.

"You've already reached your target," stated the assistant. "Everything looks perfectly normal." Jerry had reached 100 percent of his target heart rate!

Jerry wanted to yell, "Praise God," but he kept his composure.

After administering the test, a nurse asked, "Mr. Wood, there are a few more questions I need to ask for your record. Are you having chest pains?"

"No," he answered.

"Are you having shortness of breath?"

"No," he again replied.

"Are you experiencing any other discomfort?" she asked.

Again, Jerry answered, "No!"

"Then why are you here?" she questioned.

He replied, "A doctor set up the appointment, and I am only following instructions."

When Jerry got outside, however, he couldn't hide his emotions. "I ran around the parking lot and screamed for joy!" he recalled.

Previous thallium tests all recorded abnormalities in the walls of Jerry's heart. The test on April 16, 1993 records, "Normal study...."

This was the first time he ever had a normal thallium test. Even more incredible — he was off his medications at that time.

What Did You Find?

A few days later, after receiving a written report confirming that her husband's heart was perfectly normal, Kathy set up an appointment for both of them to discuss the findings with the doctor who administered the recent thallium test.

At the meeting the physician asked, "If there is no problem why did you come?"

Kathy inquired, "Didn't you find anything?"

"No. Nothing is wrong," said the doctor.

"Didn't you find that nearly half of his heart is dead?"

"Heaven's no," was the reply.

"Did you find any damaged arteries?" she questioned.

"Why are you asking?" he wanted to know.

Kathy told him about her husband's heart problems and that Jerry was to have heart bypass surgery. "The doctor began laughing and said he would have to see that in writing," she recalled.

The Woods had the complete medical files in their car and Jerry went out to get them. "He was amazed," stated Jerry "He told us, 'I've never seen a real live miracle before, but if there ever was one, this is it!'"

August 8, 1994

RE: Jerry C. Wood

To Whom It May Concern:

I am writing this letter concerning my patient, Mr. Jerry Wood, whom I have followed for ischemic coronary artery disease since 1991. He has had a previous lateral wall infarction and has had several angioplasties of the circumflex, left anterior descending and right coronary arteries. He was last admitted to the hospital in 1993 for mild, unstable angina and mild hyperlipidemia, but these problems were well controlled medically. His last thallium stress test was in February of 1994 and this showed an extremely high level of exertion at 13 minutes of a Bruce protocol with no diagnostic ST segment shifts and no clinical anginal symptoms. His nuclear scans showed only fixed lateral wall scarring without reversibility and all other areas looked to have completely normal perfusion. At this point, he appears to be extremely stable clinically with no evidence of any significant coronary obstructive disease at this time. He was released to all full, normal activities without restrictions, and at this point appears to be essentially cured since he has not had any symptoms since March of 1993. He is on a low-saturated fat, low-cholesterol diet and should maintain this indefinitely.

I hope this information is helpful in your determination, and I will be happy to provide further information as needed.

Sincerely,

DMb/kju

Jerry's doctor wrote this letter on August 8, 1994, summarizing Jerry's ordeal with heart problems. It discusses the doctor's recent findings and verifies that Jerry has not had any symptoms since the Lord powerfully came over him on March 26, 1993.

What about the doctor who had been Jerry's primary physician since the heart attack in 1991? He was doubtful at first, but on August 8, 1994, seventeen months after the miracle took place, he wrote, "Released to all full, normal activities without restrictions, and at this point appears to be essentially cured since he has not had any symptoms since March of 1993."

Jerry is still rejoicing. "From the moment of my healing I have taken no pills, had no pain, no complications — and no bypass surgery." His miracle was the subject of a news story on the local NBC affiliate television station in Evansville.

"Not only has the Lord touched me," said Jerry, "but He is also at work in the lives of Kathy, our son, Jeremy, and our entire family."

To this day Jerry still runs those 102 steps — and praises the Lord with every beat of his heart.

Lessons From
the Great Physician

Walking down the street, Jesus saw a man blind from birth. His disciples asked, "Rabbi, who sinned: this man or his parents, causing him to be born blind?"

Jesus said, "You're asking the wrong question. You're looking for someone to blame. There is no such cause-effect here. Look instead for what God can do. We need to be energetically at work for the One who sent me here, working while the sun shines. When night falls, the workday is over. For as long as I am in the world, there is plenty of light. I am the world's Light.

He said this and then spit in the dust, made a clay paste with the saliva, rubbed the paste on the blind man's eye, and said, "Go, wash at the Pool of Siloam" (Siloam means "Sent"). The man went and washed — and saw.

John 9:1-7

Jesus said, "You're asking the wrong question. You're looking for someone to blame. There is no such cause-effect here. Look instead for what God can do...."

6

This Was
Julie's Day

J ULIE, TRY TO look up!"

It was a request the little four-year-old girl had heard from her mother, Jan, countless times. Dr. Jan McClure Peel, a therapeutic optometrist, often checked the eyes of her daughter. Julie had been diagnosed with Brown's syndrome — a condition that would not allow her right eye to raise above a certain level.

The Peels live in Roma, Texas, a small community in the Rio Grande valley of South Texas, where Julie's father, John, directs a medical and missionary ministry.

"We noticed her condition at a very early age," said Jan. "Every time she tried to look at the ceiling or into the sky her left eye would lift normally, but the right eye would only reach a certain point and would not follow."

In her attempt to correct the problem, little Julie frequently tilted her head back. As she grew, her playmates began to notice, and sometimes teased her because she was "different." Julie remembered, "When I played on the gym set at the park and had to look up, my friends made fun of me." Julie's brother, Jason, would be a wonderful friend and comfort to her during those times.

The Peels grew concerned about what would happen when she entered grade school. "We knew she would have difficulty looking at the chalkboard or the screen of an overhead projector."

A Rare Condition

Jan Peel had learned a great deal about Julie's eye deficiency yet felt helpless at her inability to help her own daughter. "Brown's syndrome is so rare that I have not seen it in the five thousand patients we have treated at the clinic."

As Dr. Peel explained, "There are six muscles that control movement of our eyes. In addition to the ones that control the up, down, left and right movement, there are two muscles that actually are at angles behind the eye. One, called the inferior oblique, is underneath the eye. The other, at the top, is the superior oblique muscle — and that was the source of Julie's problem." Jan said, "It is the longest, thinnest

Juliet Elizabeth Peel

R *Oh*	L *Oh*	Primary Position	———	⬭⬭	⬭
R *Oh*	L *Oh*	Left Gaze	—————	⬭	⬭
R *Oh*	L *Oh*	Right Gaze	—————	⬭	⬭
R *slightly below midline + left cannot*	L *Oh*	Left Upward Gaze	—————	⬭	⬭
R *elevate above primary position*	L *Oh*	Straight Upward Gaze	—————	⬭	⬭
R *very slightly above primary position + right*	L	Right Upward Gaze	—————	⬭	⬭

Astanopia and diplopia on all upward gaze. Condition worsens on left upward gaze. Tilts chin upward to avoid diplopia. Age 3—supression still has not developed—probably because of infrequency of upward gaze. Measures approx. $18°-25°$ vertical imbalance.

Julie's eyes were tested for gaze positions when she was three years old. This report given November 5, 1990, diagrams the positions of her eyes when required to look in a specific direction. Notice that her left, right and straight upward gaze positions are abnormal, showing symptoms of Brown's syndrome.

muscle of the six. It attaches to the eye, goes at an angle through a small hole in the bone and attaches to the eye again and acts like a pulley to control vertical eye movement."

People with Brown's syndrome have a thickening of that long, thin muscle sheath that prohibits it from passing smoothly through the small opening in the bone. It can be caused by trauma or can be inherited.

"We are not completely certain of the source of Julie's condition, but it was noted on her birth record that she had subconjunctival hemorrhages in her right eye. It had the redness of a bloodshot eye. We decided against an operation," said Jan. "In my research, I learned that the potential complications from surgery may not warrant the risk. In some cases, children have developed a permanent problem of seeing double when reading."

When Julie turned four, she began piano lessons. "I had to explain to the teacher that she would not be able to look up at the music at the regular level," Dr. Peel stated. Julie remembered, "They either had to put the music down on the keys or sit me on a whole bunch of books."

Let's Claim It!

The Peels are a family of faith. "We always believed the Lord would one day heal Julie," said Jan. "My mother often told me, 'Julie was born this way for a purpose. It is no coincidence that you are an eye doctor and that she was born with this rare syndrome.'"

One day Jan's mother told her that when God healed Julie they would need proof. "She urged us to take a picture of her eyes — which, fortunately, we did."

It was several years ago that the Peels first heard about our ministry. "Roma didn't have a Christian cable channel, and a friend in another town sent us videos of your program to watch secondhand," said John. "There was an anointing on those tapes. We became very excited about what God was doing." They were thrilled when our daily telecasts finally reached their community on TBN (Trinity Broadcasting Network).

On Monday afternoon, February 24, 1992, Jan was cleaning the house when our program came on at 1:30. "I was doing housework, coming and going from the living room," Jan recalled. "Julie, who loved to watch *This Is Your Day,* was seated on the couch."

Near the end of the telecast, as I was praying for those who needed healing, the mother and daughter heard me say, "A right eye is being healed. Somebody's eye has just been healed by the power of Jesus."

As Jan related it, "Something just leapt in my heart, and I said, 'Did you hear that, Julie? Let's claim it!' I walked straight over to where she was sitting and touched the recess of her eye where the muscle was impeded — right on the exact spot."

"Her Eye Was Vibrating"

When Jan touched her, Julie screamed "oweee" at the top of her lungs, as if hit with a sharp pain. "I was startled because I knew it was not static electricity from the floor," said Jan. "I also knew that I had not poked her in the eye. I was just astounded. My first thought was, 'What is happening.' And my second thought was 'Oh, dear Lord, is it possible You're cutting the muscle loose?'"

At that instant, the four-year-old shouted, "It's popping, momma. It's popping!"

"What do you mean?" her mother asked.

Julie jumped to her feet, and when Jan looked at her right eye she knew exactly what her daughter meant. "Her eye was vibrating up and down vertically," stated Dr. Peel. "I couldn't believe what I was seeing. It amazed me because I knew that an eye cannot shake by itself."

So many times before, Jan had said to her daughter, "Julie, try to look up" — waiting for the moment she would be healed. Now she asked again. "At that instant Julie's eye hesitated and then was released. For the first time in four years and ten months, I watched in astonishment as both of Julie's eyes raised together in unison."

Jan continued, "It happened so fast that if I had time to dwell on it, the miracle might not have taken place. I didn't have time to doubt or to analyze. God simply did His work."

Jan fell to her knees. "I was awestruck and didn't know what to say. I felt like Thomas in New Testament times who placed his hand in the pierced side of Jesus," she states. "I had touched a miracle."

When Jason came home from school, he was so excited he continued to ask Julie to look up so he could witness the miracle again and again. "He was so amazed at what the Lord had done," said Jan.

"Like a newborn baby who learns to coordinate its

September 10, 1995

Re: Julie Peel

To: Benny Hinn Ministries

THis letter is to testify of a deficit Julie Peel had during the early years of her life. Julie was born in what appeared to be an uneventful delivery other than it was precipitous. At birth a small subconjunctival hemmorrhage was noted on physical exam but no other deficit was noted. After several years of life Julie's mother asked me if I noticed anything about Julie's eyes. An inability to look upward was noted especially with the eye adducted. The eye otherwise seemed to have normal vision. At that time we discussed the possibility of birth trauma in that the delivery was somewhat delayed due to the race to get to the hospital. Jan; Julie's mother made a tremendous effort not to push. Julie was delivered upon arrival at the hospital. We felt that perhaps attempts to delay an immenent delivery had caused pressure on that eye resulting in permanent damage to the superior oblique muscle of the right eye. The defect was noted at about 1 year and patching was attempted to strengthen the right eye to treat amblyopia.

I am not sure of the details of what happened but I can testify that Julie has normal range of motion of both eyes and there is no residual inability of upward gaze of the right eye in adduction or in any other position.

Julie Peel's mother, an optometrist, obtained this second opinion from another medical doctor. It confirms that Julie no longer has symptoms of Brown's syndrome.

eyes, Julie's eye took time for the coordination to develop completely. We continued to pray and trust in the Lord," Jan recalled. "Then she was touched again by the Lord when we attended your Little Rock, Arkansas, crusade in November 1992. Now her eye has been perfect ever since."

It's Not Small to God

Dr. Peel had a second physician examine Julie. He wrote, "Julie has normal range of motion of both eyes, and there is no residual inability of upward gaze of the right eye in adduction or in any other position."

On our telecast in January 1995, I made this statement: "If you are a doctor and you can personally verify a miracle, I would like to hear from you."

Dr. Peel heard me say those words. "I felt somewhat guilty that I had never shared Julie's healing with the Benny Hinn organization," she said. "I didn't mean to be ungrateful. We had given our testimony at our church and to many, many people. But that day I went to the eye clinic and wrote the story of how God had healed our daughter."

Julie's condition was not life-threatening, but her miracle demonstrates that the Lord is interested in every problem, from the biggest to the smallest.

Dr. Peel said, "We never know when God is going to perform a miracle. At any moment, the Lord can say, 'This is your day!'"

Lessons From the Great Physician

He came to the outskirts of Jericho. A blind man was sitting beside the road asking for handouts. When he heard the rustle of the crowd, he asked what was going on. They told him, "Jesus the Nazarene is going by."

He yelled, "Jesus! Son of David! Mercy, have mercy on me!"

Those ahead of Jesus told the man to shut up, but he only yelled all the louder, "Son of David! Mercy, have mercy on me!"

Jesus stopped and ordered him to be brought over. When he had come near, Jesus asked, "What do you want from me?"

He said, "Master, I want to see again."

Jesus said, "Go ahead — see again! Your faith has saved and healed you!" The healing was instant: He looked up, seeing — and then followed Jesus, glorifying God. Everyone in the street joined in, shouting praise to God.

Luke 18:35-43

Jesus said, "Go ahead — see again! Your faith has saved and healed you!" The healing was instant: He looked up, seeing — and then followed Jesus, glorifying God.

7

An Unexpected Touch

W"HAT ARE YOU doing home so early?" a startled Deann Scott said to her husband Ray on the afternoon of June 6, 1992. "Is something wrong?"

The thirty-year-old manager of a popular restaurant in Bakersfield, California, was proud of the fact that he had never left work early. That day, however, was different.

"Don't worry about it," he assured her, "I just need to lay down."

For two weeks the usually healthy Raymond Scott, a former sergeant in the Marines, had been feeling rather sluggish but shrugged it off. Then early that morning he began to feel an ache in his stomach that wouldn't go away. "I stayed until the lunch crowd left," he recalled, "but the pain in my abdomen was becoming severe."

"I'm taking you to the emergency room," Deann insisted, and they headed for the hospital.

"I think you're having an attack of appendicitis," the nurse on duty told Ray. Then, upon further examination, she announced, "I'm just not sure. The doctors will need to take a further look."

An Unexpected Discovery

When the physicians examined him, they felt a large mass and were greatly concerned. "Mr. Scott, we are scheduling you for immediate surgery," he was told. They didn't explain what the mass was, and Ray didn't ask. He did tell them, however, that he was allergic to anesthesia so they used a spinal block to kill the pain.

Ray was on the operating table much longer than expected. What the two surgeons discovered was not good news. They found a tumor that was so large it had literally eaten up his healthy appendix and left a hole in his nearby intestines. The pain he felt was from the gangrene and peritonitis that had set in as the appendix and nearby intestines began to rot.

The tumor engulfed the colon at the juncture of the large and small intestine. The doctors removed the tumor by taking out part of his intestines and adjacent lymph nodes and sewed him up.

Two days later, Ray Scott and his wife were in his hospital room watching Michael Landon's TV series,

Highway to Heaven. The episode was the story of a young lady who learns she has cancer. "We had just turned the television set off when one of the surgeons walked into the room," he recalled. "In a very matter-of-fact manner, he told me, 'Mr. Scott, we have examined the tissues very carefully, and you need to know that you have cancer.'"

Ray learned that the malignant tumor had also ruptured, spraying seedling-like cells throughout the right lower area of his abdomen. A lymph node had also tested positive, and the doctors knew he was in trouble.

When the surgeon left the room, Ray and Deann just held each other and cried. That same week, the tumor board of the hospital met, and Ray's case was on the agenda. The board consisted of a group of radiologists, oncologists, surgeons and general practitioners.

What was their collective prognosis? The board discussed the possibility of giving Ray whole abdominal radiation as a precaution to kill any cancer that may have spread. Unfortunately because of the dose and the need to protect his liver and kidneys from the radiation, doctors ruled out this plan. Their final recommendation was to begin chemotherapy and limited radiation treatment.

Ray could hardly bear to think of the future. Tears welled again when he thought about his two beautiful daughters, Lindsey and Ashley, who were only six and nine years old.

Immediately, Ray began five weeks of radiation treatments. He also started chemotherapy.

One year later a series of abdominal operations were begun. First, on March 5, 1993, there was the removal of a blockage in his small intestine. "I was growing weary of instant oatmeal and liquid food," he recalled.

At the same time an additional three feet of intestine was removed, showing more cancer. Plus another lymph node tested positive for cancer.

What Is Happening?

Seven months later, while he and his wife were at home one evening, Ray exclaimed, "Look at this!" Suddenly, the side of his stomach seemed to roll as if something was pressing against it from the inside, and Ray began to experience pain. Frightened, they rushed to the hospital. It was a painful hernia that had developed in the area of the scar from his prior surgery.

Ray was immediately scheduled for a third surgery because of the nature of a painful hernia. A hernia is caused by intestine protruding into a weakness in the abdominal wall. Pain in a hernia indicates that the abdominal muscles are cutting off the blood supply to the intestine. This can cause that portion of the intestine to die and produce gangrene, which could result in death. Had Ray not gone to the hospital and had surgery, his life could have been in serious danger.

Again, as in the previous operations, they spotted more cancer and attempted to remove what they could. "They even found it in the muscles of my back," he related.

What was the result of the chemotherapy? "It was

holding the problem at bay," he stated. "But the cells that were already affected were producing tumors."

In February 1994, for the fourth time in twenty months, Ray faced another surgery. "To the doctor's dismay, I developed a blockage of my right ureter, the tube that carries urine from the right kidney to the bladder," recalled Ray. "It was such a serious matter that I signed papers stating they could remove the kidney if the problem could not be resolved."

The procedure was a success, but it also revealed that the blockage was a cluster of cancer cells. In addition to this they also found cancer invading the muscles of his back. During the operation, the surgeon also installed a port-a-cath, a catheter device placed directly into the large vein beneath the collar bone. This was to make it easier to give Ray chemotherapy. "After a year and a half of the chemo, my veins had not reacted well. They needed another way to get the treatment into my system," he said.

"I'm afraid we're going to have to treat this more aggressively," his doctor told him. Ray's primary physician is an outstanding Christian who inspired Ray's faith but at the same time faced reality.

First there were half-hour treatments once a week. Then two hours a week. It eventually increased to an eight-hour weekly session, plus a twenty-four-hour waist pack, a pump that put slow-release chemotherapy into Ray night and day. "I wore it everywhere: in bed, in the shower. I never took it out, except to refill it once a week," he states.

That same month, Ray's illness forced him to stop working. "Before that time, I would periodically take a month off to recover and then return to the restaurant," he explained. Now that had become impossible.

Is It Really Easter?

The Scotts received tremendous love and support from the members of their church, and Ray was especially looking forward to Easter with his wife and the girls.

"I can't begin to tell you how devastated I was the day after Good Friday when I began to have severe upper back and neck pains and could hardly move," he said. "On Easter morning my doctor immediately admitted me to the hospital. They feared that my spinal cord was being compressed. Thankfully it was not. Tests showed I was also passing a large amount of protein in my urine. Because of that they performed a kidney biopsy. During the hospital stay, the left side of my neck, my left shoulder, arm and hand swelled up to what seemed about three times their normal size," he remembered. The cause was a massive blood clot in the vein under Ray's collar bone.

Ray's parents flew from New Jersey to Bakersfield to visit him. His mother had been a nurse all of her adult life. She took one look at her son and thought to herself, "It's not going to be long." She had seen patients in that condition before.

Ray was raised in a Catholic family and had always been active in church. In the Marine Corps one of his fellow marines, a born-again Christian, challenged Ray's faith. As a result of their discussions, one night in his bunkhouse Ray prayed, "Jesus, I ask You to come into my heart and be the Lord of my life." The

Lord answered his prayer, and his faith continued to develop and grow.

Choices

In August 1994, Ray faced another life-threatening situation when he was hospitalized for a second blood clot. Doctors found the clot in a major vein in his neck. If that clot had broken loose, it could have gone to his brain, causing a stroke, or traveled to his heart and pushed into his lungs. If it had reached Ray's lungs and stopped blood exchange, it could have proven to be fatal.

"Since I had already gone through four operations, radiation therapy and chemotherapy and was still alive, I felt that somehow I would survive the blood clots, too," said Ray. And he did.

Yet his cancer crisis continued. In October 1994, Ray's doctor suggested he have another oncoscint scan — a test that uses radioactive tracers by injecting them into the patient. The tracers seek out molecules unique to cancer cells. Then the tracers attach to the infected cells, and when a scan is done these areas "light up" on the scan. The scan Ray had was indicative of recurrent disease and suspicious for metastatic (cancer) disease. It confirmed the doctor's fears — cancer remained.

Ray's doctor told him, "I can't talk remission. I can't talk recovery. All I can discuss with you is quality of life." He continued, "Ray, you have one of two choices: You can either go on a more intense chemo, which you need to do; or we can try some other form, and you can go back to work. That's what I know you really want to do." Then he added, "Either way, it doesn't look good."

Before making any decisions there was something Ray had to take care of.

Earlier that year Ray made plans to take his wife on a cruise during the first week of November. It was a rather improbable goal, but something he had promised her for their tenth wedding anniversary. Besides, it was her birthday.

Only two days after being released from the hospital, this time for abdominal pain, Ray took a step of faith and went on the cruise. "We sailed down the Pacific coast toward Mexico. It was as if I was suspended in time," he recalled. "That entire week I was pain-free."

When the Scotts returned, they were invited to come to Sacramento where our ministry was conducting a crusade in the Arco Arena.

Reaching Out

"The day we were to leave for Sacramento it seemed all my symptoms returned. I was having pain and problems with short bowel syndrome [a condition causing loose bowels] and was extremely weak," he recalled. All the way to the crusade, Ray was looking for the nearest hospital, knowing that at any moment he might need to make a detour.

In order to find a good seat, Ray and Deann Scott arrived at the arena mid-afternoon on November 16, 1994. Being in pain, he sought out an usher who came and personally prayed with him.

Before the service started, the Scotts made friends with an eighteen-year-old girl who brought

OPERATIVE REPORT

DATE OF OPERATION: 06/07/92

PREOPERATIVE DIAGNOSIS: Acute appendicitis.

POSTOPERATIVE DIAGNOSIS: Acute perforated appendicitis with
                               obstruction of the ileocecal valve.

OPERATION: 1. Exploratory laparotomy.
                               2. Partial right hemicolectomy.

Anesthesia: Spinal.

DESCRIPTION OF OPERATION: The patient's abdomen was scrubbed
with Betadine for 10 minutes.

With the patient in the supine position under spinal anesthesia,
a transverse incision was made in the right lower quadrant of
the abdomen.   Subcutaneous bleeders were clamped and
electrocoagulated.   The external oblique fascia was opened in a
transverse fashion.   The internal oblique muscles were split
bluntly in the direction of their fibers.   The peritoneum was
tented up and opened with sharp dissection.   A large mass was
present involving almost the entire right lower quadrant of the
abdomen. With a great deal of difficulty, the mass was worked
up into the wound.   The mass involved the terminal ileum and
cecum and was freed from the right retroperitoneum and gutter
with blunt and sharp dissection.

Inspection of the mass revealed a probable perforated appendix.
The appendix itself could actually not be found. Only fragments
on the back of the cecum could be seen.   A large hole was
present which was assumed to be the tract of the appendix
leading into the cecum.   There was a massive inflammatory
response throughout the cecum and terminal ileum. The ileocecal
valve could not be identified.   It was felt that there was
possible obstruction secondary to the inflammatory mass.   The
terminal ileum was transected with the GIA stapling device as
was the cecum just above the area of the inflammatory mass.   The
mesentery, including all the inflammatory tissue was serially

(CONTINUED)

This surgical report of June 7, 1992, shows doctors discovered
a large tumor that had eaten up Ray's appendix. Note the report
states, "the appendix itself could not actually be found."
This was the beginning of Ray's battle with cancer.

her five-week-old daughter for healing. The infant had Down's syndrome plus two holes in her little heart.

Ray's thoughts prior to the crusade were, "Lord, just give me the strength to go through a more intense round of chemo and to do whatever You want me to do." He wasn't really thinking of his own healing.

As the meeting began and the music filled the vast auditorium, Ray became overwhelmed with a desire to pray for the child with Down's syndrome. He was so focused on the need that at one point Ray took the hand of the baby and prayed, "Lord, please don't ever take this child's life. Take mine!"

A powerful anointing was present in the service that night. Ray describes what happened. "As I prayed for that little child, it felt as if the Holy Spirit went right through me. I could feel something electrifying penetrate my own incision, and I felt I was a conduit to that child."

Then, just as Ray released the hand of the baby, the same usher who had prayed for Ray earlier stepped up to him and asked, "Do you remember me? Do you feel any different than when you came in?"

Ray, astounded that the usher could find him in a crowd of eighteen thousand people, replied, "Yes. The pain is gone." Everything else seemed to be returning to normal instantly. Ray said, "I reached down to feel my abdomen where I earlier felt two hernias developing. They had disappeared!"

The usher walked Ray over to a medical doctor who spoke with him, and a few seconds later, he was on the platform with me. Ray said, "I didn't realize it,

CASE SUMMARY

Re: Raymond Scott

Mr. Scott is a 33 year-old man that I initially met in June of 1993. This was slightly more than one year following his diagnosis of the colon. This diagnosis had been established in the previous year in June at which time Mr. Scott had presented to the emergency department with acute abdominal pain and was thought to have acute appendicitis. At the time of operation, Mr. Scott was found to have a large adenocarcinoma at the ileocecal valve as well as a ruptured appendix with extensive peritonitis. A partial right hemicolectomy was performed. A large primary tumor measuring 6.5 cm. in greatest dimension was removed as well as one lymph node. Postoperatively, Mr. Scott was given chemotherapy with 5-FU and Levamisole as well as localized radiation.

Follow-up colonoscopy in December of 1992 was unremarkable, and further restaging studies did not show evidence of cancer. However, Mr. Scott developed abdominal symptomatology in February of 1993 prompting a repeat evaluation. At that time, colonoscopy revealed a marked narrowing of the primary anastomosis and an exploratory procedure revealed a locally recurrent tumor near the anastomosis. Tumor was also involving lymph nodes at that time, and a much larger resection was carried out. Further analysis at that time revealed involvement not only of the colon but also of the small bowel and local soft tissues in the anterior peritoneal wall. No evidence of extra abdominal metastasis were identified.

The patient was continued on chemotherapy but had further abdominal difficulties requiring another exploratory laparotomy performed in October of 1993. At that time, he demonstrated a significant decrease in disease but some residual. A further change in chemotherapy was accomplished at that time, but with significant diminishment in his quality of life. After continuing on chemotherapy until February, the patient had evidence of further recurrence after developing a right ureteral obstruction with hydronephrosis. He had a further recurrence at that time and this was resected. Postoperatively, his chemotherapy was changed to 5-FU and Cis-platinum.

Follow-up CT scans in May showed no evidence of disease and an oncoscint scan was requested at that time. This showed activity in the abdomen consistent with residual disease and an adjustment was made in his treatment. This was interrupted several times because of infection and portacath thrombosis. Restaging was accomplished in late October with a stable oncoscint scan at that time and no other evidence of disease.

Plans to modify therapy were made, but before this was instituted, Mr. Scott experienced a miraculous healing. Since that time, Mr. Scott has been doing extremely well and without clinical evidence of active disease. He has been able to return to work as well as to all normal activities following this amazing recovery.

This case summary on Ray Scott describes the scope of his problems through his bout with cancer. Notice his doctor states: "Ray experienced a miraculous healing...[and] has been doing extremely well...."

but right behind me was my wife and my mother-in-law. They knew exactly when the Lord touched me. They could feel it, too."

As Ray stood before me on that stage, the Lord impressed on me to say, "God's power is all over you. There's a miracle happening to you!"

I put one hand on Ray's back and the other on his stomach and literally pushed on it. Ray said, "Where my abdomen had been soft, it became rock solid as if the Lord had put a strap or something over the incision. I knew it immediately."

The Physician's Conclusion

The next morning Ray called his doctor from a pay phone in the lobby of the Arco Arena. He recalls, "I couldn't get through to him, so I left a message on his voice mail saying, 'I'm healed!' The nurses didn't know what to make of the message, but the doctor did. He couldn't wait to see me."

When Ray returned to Bakersfield he told his physician, "I need to take that oncoscint scan again." He wanted to document his healing so he could avoid more chemotherapy. The expensive exam had just been given the previous month, and it took a great deal of persuasion to convince the insurance company to pay for the administration of it again. But they agreed.

However, there was only one problem. As a result of the previous oncoscint scan, Ray's body produced certain antibodies that would not allow the administration of the test again. When the doctors told him this, Ray decided to stand in faith and not continue chemotherapy.

Ray took other blood tests to monitor his condition, but he remembered with excitement, "My pain was all gone."

I rejoiced with Ray when I read the written report from his surgeon dated February 28, 1995: "At the present time, he has no evidence of recurrence of cancer within his body. He now has the ability to stand as a testament to his faith and religion."

What was Ray doing a month after his healing? He was helping to install seventy heavy wooden pews in the church he attends. "My strength returned immediately!" he said.

It's been more than a year now since the Lord miraculously healed Raymond Scott, and Ray stands in faith every day that his cancer will not recur. He has not had any chemotherapy since the Lord touched him, and his blood tests for cancer levels have normalized. Ray's doctor wrote, "Mr. Scott experienced a miraculous healing. Since that time, Mr. Scott has been doing extremely well and without clinical evidence of active disease. He has been able to return to work as well as to all normal activities following this amazing recovery.

Ray is now managing high-volume restaurants for major companies. He concluded, "In our place of business we serve hundreds of customers every day, but nothing can ever compare with how the Lord has served me. And I'm continually praising Him for it!"

Lessons From the Great Physician

Jesus said, "Let's go to the rest of the villages so I can preach there also. This is why I've come." He went to their meeting places all through Galilee, preaching and throwing out the demons.

A leper came to him, begging on his knees, "If you want to, you can cleanse me."

Deeply moved, Jesus put out his hand, touched him, and said, "I want to. Be clean." Then and there the leprosy was gone, his skin smooth and healthy. Jesus dismissed him with strict orders: "Say nothing to anyone. Take the offering for cleansing that Moses prescribed and present yourself to the priest. This will validate your healing to the people." But as soon as the man was out of earshot, he told everyone he met what had happened, spreading the news all over town.

Mark 1:38-45

A leper came to him, begging on his knees, "If you want to, you can cleanse me." Deeply moved, Jesus put out his hand, touched him, and said, "I want to. Be clean."

8

Brenda's Deep, Deep Valley

W HAT'S GOING WRONG?" thought thirty-
seven-year-old Brenda Forgy. "Why do my emotions
seem to be coming apart at the seams?"

Before long the Orlando, Florida, woman's concern
was for more than her emotions. "I began to experience abnormal menstrual cycles and didn't know how
to respond to the unusual feelings in my body."

When she told her husband, Dennis, what was happening, he immediately insisted that she make an
appointment to see her doctor.

Brenda's examination on August 9, 1988, determined
that she had a serious imbalance in her hormones. Her

Janice Fuchs enjoys a relaxing day in the park with her son Gabor and her dog, Tootsie.

Janice enjoys working out with weights in a neighborhood gym — using arms and hands that had been painful and useless prior to her healing from Reflex Sympathetic Dystrophy (RSD).

Timmy Ballard is a normal, healthy, energetic thirteen-year-old since he experienced his day for a miracle (picture taken January 11, 1996).

Timmy demonstrates his skill and endurance at inline skating — impossible before he was healed from a rare blood disease.

Jerry Wood and his wife, Kathy, surrender their lives to the Lord on March 26, 1993, during a morning service at a miracle crusade. That evening God healed Jerry of heart blockage.

Jerry's face radiates his joy and good health (picture taken October 10, 1995).

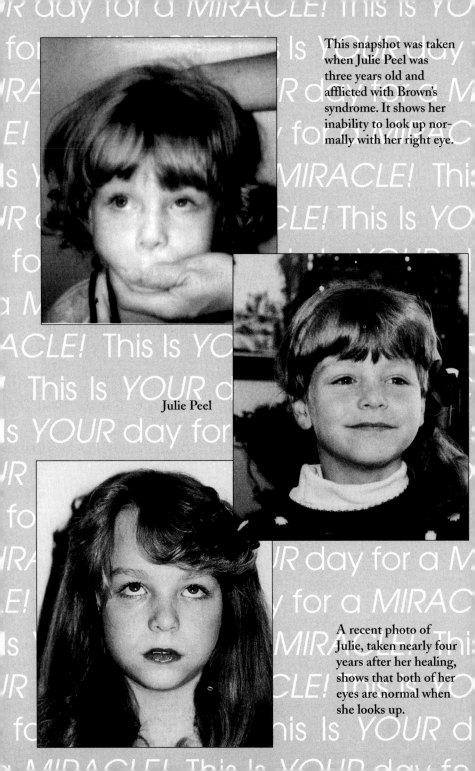

This snapshot was taken when Julie Peel was three years old and afflicted with Brown's syndrome. It shows her inability to look up normally with her right eye.

Julie Peel

A recent photo of Julie, taken nearly four years after her healing, shows that both of her eyes are normal when she looks up.

Pictured is Ray Scott with his mother-in-law, Myra; his wife, Deann; and two daughters, Lindsey and Ashley.

Ray and his twin brother, Roger, enjoy being outdoors together after Ray's cancer went into remission.

This picture of Brenda Forgy with her husband and children was taken several months after the tumor on her pituitary gland disappeared (picture taken February 1993).

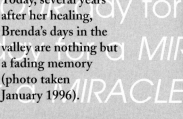

Today, several years after her healing, Brenda's days in the valley are nothing but a fading memory (photo taken January 1996).

RIGHT: This is some of the medical equipment Pat Harrington used during five years of disability.

MIDDLE: Pat radiates peace after her healing from peroneal nerve palsy, left knee instability and right shoulder dislocation.

Pat and her husband, Allen, return her medical equipment to the suppliers. When she first received the brace she carries, she told the supplier, "It's only temporary — Jesus is a healer."

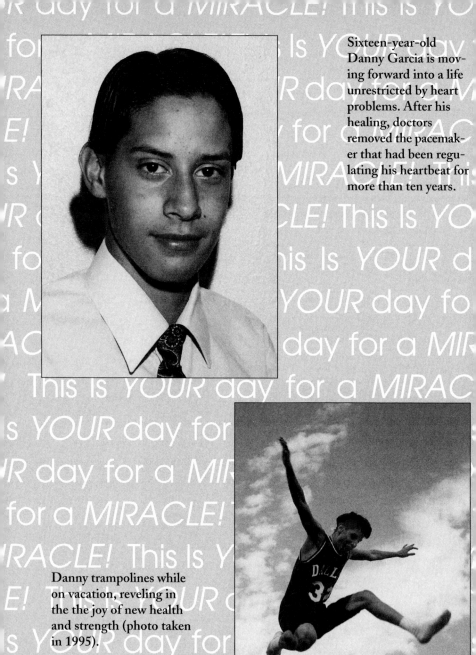

Sixteen-year-old Danny Garcia is moving forward into a life unrestricted by heart problems. After his healing, doctors removed the pacemaker that had been regulating his heartbeat for more than ten years.

Danny trampolines while on vacation, reveling in the the joy of new health and strength (photo taken in 1995).

Suzanne Frick heads back to work to drive a truck with her husband, Alan, and she's feeling great. The back pain caused by a disk injury is gone (photo taken October 13, 1995).

Just two weeks before she attends the crusade where she was healed, Suzanne lays on a couch in great pain, unable to climb the stairs to her bed (photo taken April 26, 1995).

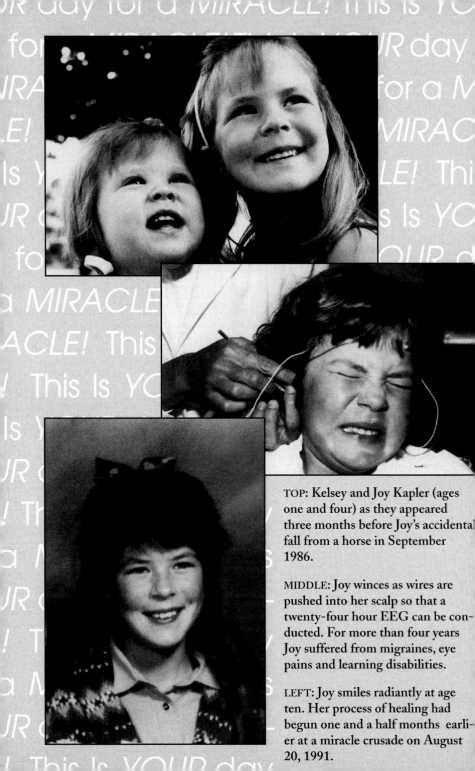

TOP: Kelsey and Joy Kapler (ages one and four) as they appeared three months before Joy's accidental fall from a horse in September 1986.

MIDDLE: Joy winces as wires are pushed into her scalp so that a twenty-four hour EEG can be conducted. For more than four years Joy suffered from migraines, eye pains and learning disabilities.

LEFT: Joy smiles radiantly at age ten. Her process of healing had begun one and a half months earlier at a miracle crusade on August 20, 1991.

Joy Kapler at age fifteen leads a normal, healthy life.

The Kapler family (from left): Kelsey, Rich, Joy and
Theresa.

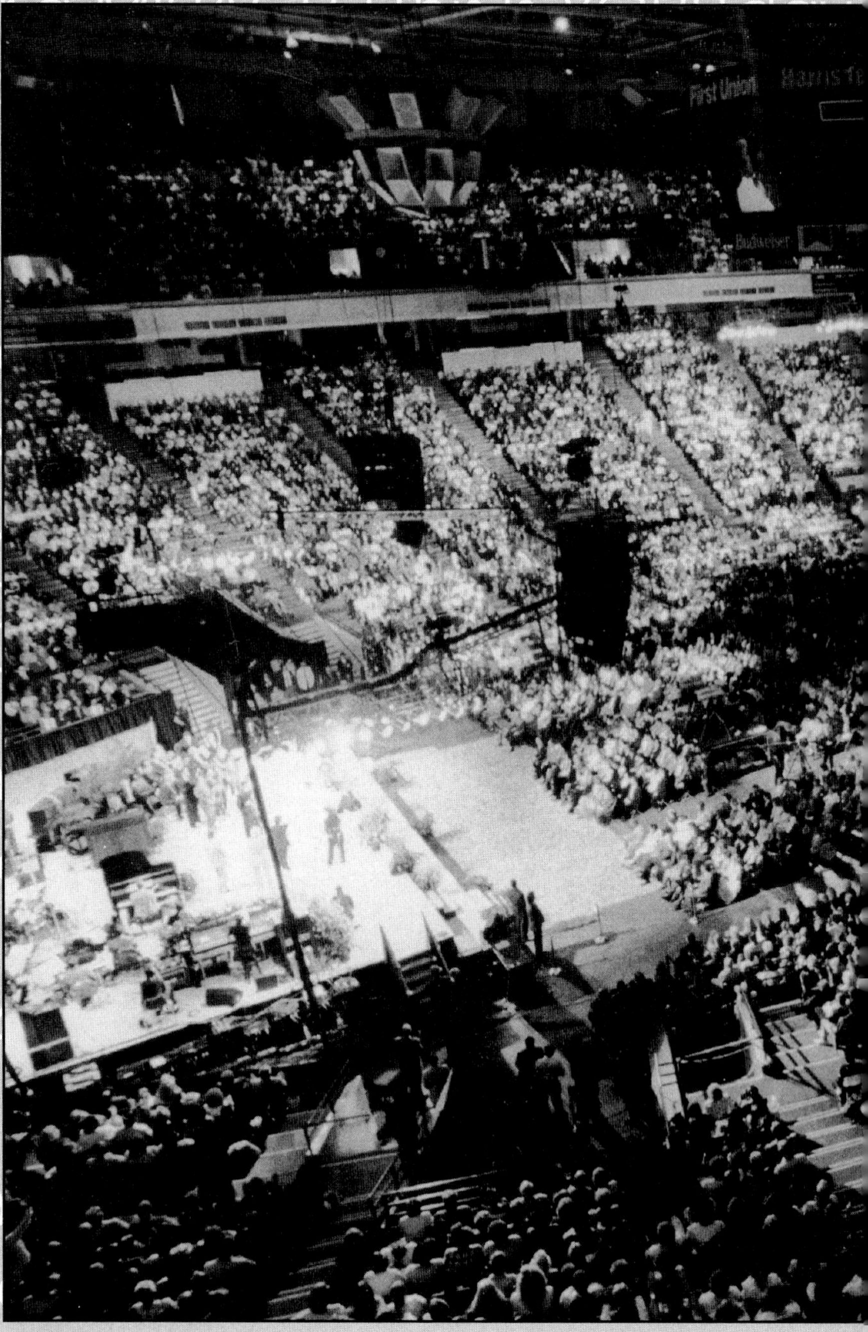

for a *MIRACLE!* This Is *YOUR*

The Charlotte Miracle Crusade at the Charlotte Coliseum
(North Carolina). The seating capacity was twenty-three thousand.

Benny Hinn proclaims the power of God
to save, heal and transform lives as he
mnisters at crusades worldwide.

This picture captures a thrilling moment as God grants healing to a man attending a miracle crusade.

This Is *YOUR* day for a *MIRACLE!*

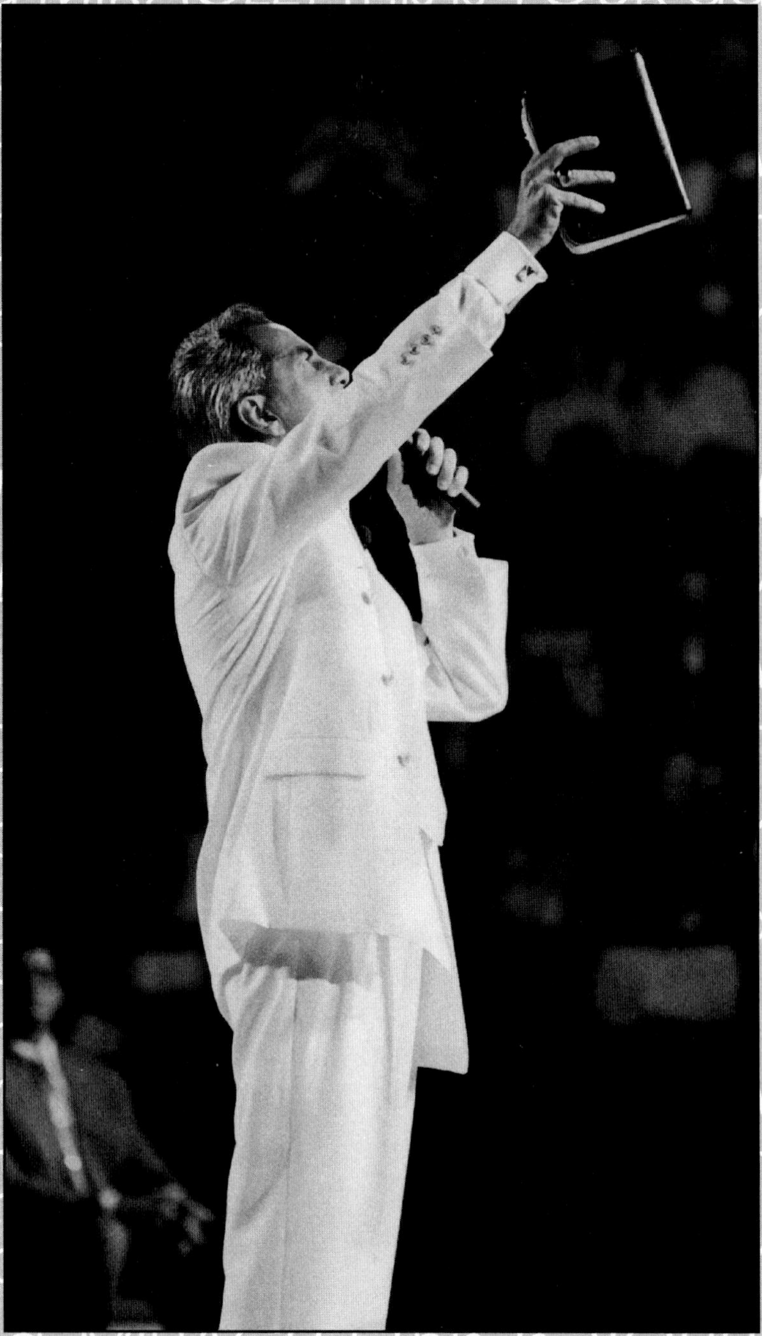

prolactin hormone count was very high. At this time the doctor ordered a CT scan and the results revealed the cause of her problem. "You have a tumor on your pituitary," reported the physician. "It looks like something you have had for some time."

The pituitary is a pea-sized gland that hangs from the base of the brain, just below the optic nerves. The pituitary regulates the activities of most of the endocrine glands. These glands release vital hormones directly into the bloodstream. Brenda learned that even a benign, noncancerous tumor of the pituitary can cause serious disorders by disturbing the flow of hormones.

Immediately her doctor prescribed Parlodel to try to keep the tumor from growing. "It may be something you can live with, and hopefully the tumor will not grow," the doctor said.

However, the prescribed medicine produced unwanted side effects. "I was having such negative reactions that I couldn't continue to take the medicine," she recalled. "My sinuses swelled up, and my nasal passages closed. Plus, the medicine made me nauseous day after day."

When she complained to her physician, he explained, "This is the only medication that will retard the growth of the adenoma [tumor]. I'll cut the prescription down, but you really need to keep taking it."

Over the next year Brenda continued to struggle with the medication. She finally stopped taking it because she couldn't bear the side effects. Meanwhile Brenda's mood swings continued, and additional complications began to emerge. "I began having milk in my breasts as well as headaches and was close to a total emotional breakdown," she recalled. "It affected my job and my home life. And because I suffered, every member of our family suffered."

The Risky Options

In 1991, the results of an MRI were not encouraging. The doctor prepared Brenda for the possibility of surgery. She was warned that if the tumor became much larger it could press on the optic nerve and damage her vision.

Brenda saw a neurosurgeon who gave her the details of the surgery she could be facing. "He explained that it was very delicate micro-surgery through my nasal passage, and that a hole would likely be drilled in the back of my skull to reach the pituitary," said Brenda. "He also warned me of all the things that could go wrong — including the possibility that I could go blind if the surgery did not go well." There was also the chance of the subsequent need for hormonal replacement therapy.

Sudden Pain

Because of complications from the tumor, Brenda's estrogen level was also low. Her doctor prescribed an Estraderm patch on June 5, 1992. Brenda applied it as instructed.

On June 17, Brenda began to have a severe headache. She had never had a headache like this before. "It had become so bad that I stayed in bed for several days," she recalled. To help relieve the problem her physician arranged for her to have an injection for pain relief at a local clinic. The clinic doctor wondered if the patch had caused Brenda's headache, so she removed it. But the pain persisted.

On Sunday afternoon, June 21, Brenda's torment was almost more than she could bear. "I had received one shot, yet felt I needed to return to the clinic because the sharp pain in the back of my head was so great. It felt like I was being stabbed with a knife."

Brenda asked her sixteen-year-old son, Eric, to take her to the clinic. When they arrived, the waiting room was so crowded she knew the stay would be lengthy. Brenda was in such pain she turned to Eric and said, "Oh, just take me on to church."

For the past several years, Brenda had been a member of our church in Orlando, now called World Outreach Center. "Week after week I believed for my healing and claimed God's promises," she recalled.

Brenda was at the low point of a deep, deep valley but she continued to hold onto the Word that says "by His stripes we are healed" (Is. 53:5, NKJV). She also remembered reading a book advising her that Scripture is like medicine — it needs to be taken three times a day. "I was doing that," she stated.

It was about 4:30 in the afternoon when Brenda arrived at the church. The service didn't begin until six o'clock, but the auditorium was already well filled. "I didn't usually sit near the front, but that day I felt compelled to get as close to the platform as I could," remembered Brenda. "A lady a few rows from the front, who was aware of my illness, saw me and scooted over, 'We can make room for you,' she said."

THIS IS YOUR DAY FOR A MIRACLE

Brenda apologized for being so sick and hoped the woman would understand if she had to suddenly leave the auditorium.

During the meeting that night, a woman who had been to the previous healing service gave a special testimony that greatly inspired Brenda's faith. At that point in the service, Brenda began to reach out for her own healing. "There was an atmosphere of anointing that seemed to lift me above my problems. I began to believe — *really* believe — I was going to be healed."

Brenda began to feel an unusual heat in her body. It didn't suddenly come and then leave — the warmth remained as the service continued.

Next, in an unforgettable moment, the Lord was especially real to Brenda. "Pastor Benny, you said, 'Right now I want you to cry out to God and ask for your healing!'" she recalled. "And that's when I felt the Lord doing a special work in me."

Brenda did not go the platform, and no one specifically prayed over her. She simply reached out to the Lord, and He heard her cry. The stabbing pain in the back of her head immediately disappeared, even though the rest of her head still ached. "It felt as if I had hurt myself and there was still some soreness, but the excruciating pain was gone."

After the service, the woman seated next to Brenda turned and asked, "How do you feel?"

"It's gone," she replied. "The pain is gone from the back of my head."

Since Brenda's husband had not been with her in the service that night, she called for him to pick her

FORGY, BRENDA   STAT:N
00172 43 02   SEX:F AGE:
DOCTOR:
DATE/TIME COLLECTED:07/16/92 11:20   BY:
DATE/TIME REPORTED: 07/17/92 13:00

	PATIENT RESULT						
TEST	LOW	NORMAL	HIGH	UNITS	EXPECTED	RANGE	TECH
PROLACTN		4.8		NG/ML	0.1	- 20.0	DP

The results of this hormone test dated July 18, 1992 — one month after Brenda experienced a healing touch from God — show her prolactin count had returned to a normal range. This favorable report prompted doctors to postpone plans for surgery.

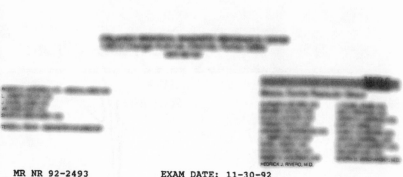

MR NR 92-2493   EXAM DATE: 11-30-92
FORGY, BRENDA   DOB: 11-23-47
ROBERT BOWLES, M. D.   RM: OUT-PATIENT

MRI OF THE SELLA:

Contrast was given I.V. and then 3D acquired 3 mm. scans were made
across the sella in sagittal and coronal planes. Scans show normal
sellar contents – no sellar mass is present. Suprasellar cisterns
are normal.

Scans from 06-12-92 show a large mass in the sella with deviation
of the pituitary stalk sharply to the right. Enhancing tissue
along the right side of the sella on the earlier study is probably
the normal gland. The only sign of this mass seen now is slight
residual tilt of the pituitary stalk toward the right side.

CONCLUSION: **MASS SEEN IN THE SELLA ON STUDY OF 06-12-92 IS
                 GONE.**

ROBERT D. ANDERSON, M. D.
12-01-92/DJM

The results of a test on November 30, 1992, show that
the pituitary mass seen five-and-a-half months earlier
was no longer there.

up. She hopped in the car and said, "Dennis, let's stop and get something to eat on the way home."

She was surprised by her own words. "I had not been able to eat in three days, and suddenly my appetite returned. The next morning, I felt my energy level beginning to bounce back," she recalled.

Seeing the Physician

The following day Brenda saw her doctor. He reviewed the MRI results from the scan completed earlier in the month. It had shown that the adenoma had a small increase in size. The doctor had discussed surgery with her on that occasion.

Because Brenda's physician had recommended surgery on her pituitary, she had already scheduled an appointment with another neurosurgeon which was to take place a few days later. Since she was seeking a second opinion, she didn't want to cancel the meeting.

The neurosurgeon reviewed Brenda's past history and the MRIs. He discussed the risks of surgery and what it could do to Brenda. Brenda told him about her severe headache and how it had gone away after coming to a healing service.

He recommended she and her husband discuss the possibility of two alternatives: She could undergo surgery; or she could wait and see if the tumor would shrink with menopause or as a result of what had happened nine days earlier

She returned to her original doctor and told him about her healing. "I have not felt better in years," she said.

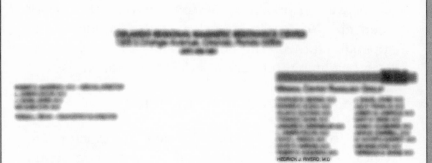

MR NR 94-0691   EXAM DATE: 02-04-94
FORGY, BRENDA   DOB: 11-23-47
PETER PERRY, M. D.   RM: OUT-PATIENT

MRI OF THE BRAIN and SELLA:

Plain sagittal and coronal scans were made first. These studies show no abnormality around the sella or through the center of the cerebrum generally. Contrast material was then given I.V. after which 3D acquired 3 mm. scans were made centered on the sella. Studies show no mass or abnormal tissue enhancement. The pituitary stalk tilts slightly toward the right but there is no mass on the left. Findings are identical to 11-30-92.

CONCLUSION: NO EVIDENCE FOR PITUITARY MASS.

Almost two years after Brenda received her healing, yet another test on February 4, 1994, revealed that the pituitary mass had disappeared.

He tested Brenda's prolactin level on July 16, 1992. She was not surprised at the results. "They are better than normal," he informed her. An eye exam was also normal. Brenda and her doctor decided to postpone surgery indefinitely.

The physician eventually ordered another MRI which was conducted on November 30, 1992. By this time Brenda's life had returned to normal, and she was working full-time at a job in merchandising. "I was in Gainesville, Florida, when I stopped at a pay phone to talk to the doctor. I was anxious to learn the results of the MRI," she said.

The physician told his rejuvenated patient, "You're not going to believe this, but it's not there anymore. There is no tumor — no lump on your pituitary."

On February 4, 1994, the findings of yet another MRI were identical to the previous November test. The medical report states, "No evidence for pituitary mass."

Brenda's days in the valley are a fading memory. She smiled, "The Lord has given me a view from the mountain, and I will never stop praising Him."

Lessons From the Great Physician

A woman who had suffered a condition of hemorrhaging for twelve years — a long succession of physicians had treated her, and treated her badly, taking all her money and leaving her worse off than before — had heard about Jesus. She slipped in from behind and touched his robe. She was thinking to herself, "If I can put a finger on his robe, I can get well." The moment she did it, the flow of blood dried up. She could feel the change, and knew her plague was over and done with.

At the same moment, Jesus felt energy discharging from him. He turned around to the crowd and asked, "Who touched my robe?"

His disciples said..."You're asking, 'Who touched me?' Dozens have touched you!"

But he went on asking, looking around to see who had done it. The woman, knowing what had happened, knowing she was the one, stepped up in fear and trembling, knelt before him, and gave him the whole story.

Jesus said to her, "Daughter, you took a risk of faith, and now you're healed and whole. Live well, live blessed! Be healed of your plague."

Mark 5:25-34

Jesus said to her, "Daughter, you
took a risk of faith, and now you're healed
and whole. Live well, live blessed!"

9

Walking in Worcester

IT WAS A hot summer day in northern Vermont in 1950. Seven-year-old Patricia was singing as she ran beside a tractor and manure spreader in a neighbor's cornfield.

"Suddenly I was caught by one of the extensions that was attached to the tractor. It went across me diagonally and the farmer continued up field until he realized I was not running with him anymore," she recalled.

Finally the farmer saw Patricia in the field and rushed to her side. The little girl's pelvis and one lung were crushed and her left ear was severely damaged. Yet in her state of shock, she continued singing.

There were no doctors available in this rural area near Milton, about thirty miles from the Canadian border, so they called a local veterinarian who rushed to the farm.

Paralyzed from the waist down, they placed Patricia's crumpled body in a galvanized metal tub and carried her to the house before driving her to the nearest hospital. "At the hospital, I was immediately put in traction and began a long rehabilitation process," said Patricia.

The doctors questioned whether she would ever be able to have children or even walk again, but the feeling finally came back to Patricia's legs. When she took her first steps, however, it was obvious that she had a permanent injury as she began dragging the left side of her body. She was unable to be active in any school sports.

During the years that followed, Patricia was constantly falling — adding complications to her injuries and often putting her back in the hospital. "Once I fell on the marble steps at school and put my hips out of their sockets." At Belows Free Academy in St. Albans, she was known as "the one with the limp."

Searching for an Exit

Patricia was married at the age of seventeen and within the next few years bore five sons — three of which had rather serious birth defects. One son was born with a badly deformed leg and only a stump for a foot.

As the years passed, her marriage, which had been extremely unstable, totally fell apart. At the age of thirty-two, no longer able to cope with life, she said to herself, "Stop the world. I want to get off."

Patricia's oldest son had been diagnosed with epilepsy and given a prescription for phenobarbital. Because of an allergic reaction, he was unable to take the medication. "I saved a large supply of those pills with the idea that I could use them to end my life," Patricia said.

In a half-empty apartment in Burlington, Vermont, with more problems than any mother should face, a desperate Patricia took a sheet of paper and wrote, "Hell could not be worse than this pain I am going through. If this does not work, I will find a gun and make sure it works the next time." She then swallowed a huge quantity of phenobarbital — more than enough to kill the average person.

She was found by her youngest son, laying unconscious on the floor. An ambulance rushed her to the hospital. The effects of the overdose were devastating — all of her systems shut down. The hospital did everything in their power to save her. "When I finally regained consciousness, my emotions were raw, and I was angry that I was alive," she confessed.

Patricia had to learn to walk again, and how to use her arms and hands. "I could not feed myself or control the wheelchair they gave me. My body had blisters from head to toe, inside and out. The overdose had burned my throat, making it almost impossible for me to speak."

A New Beginning

While in that hospital an elderly patient nearby

came to her bed and gave her a book unlike anything she had ever received. It was *Seed Faith,* written by Oral Roberts.

"The man died shortly after giving me the book," she said, "but his last act of kindness was a gift of life."

It was the first Christian book she had ever read. Patricia had been raised in a Catholic home, and her parents did their best to instill good moral and ethical values, but the family rarely attended church. Now, in her valley of despair, she began turning to God's Word to find answers. "The Bible spoke directly to me," she said. "And I asked Christ to cleanse my heart of sin. Again and again I asked the Lord to forgive me for trying to take my own life. I realized that suicide was wrong."

Two years later, in 1975, the Lord sent Allen Harrington into Patricia's life — someone she had known from high school days. Soon they were married. He became a devoted Christian. He worked for a major computer company and together they established a Christ-centered home.

Although her physical problems continued throughout the years, her new-found faith and the support of Allen gave her tremendous strength. Patricia's personal life was restored, and she now had a reason to look forward to life.

The Downward Spiral

In October 1989, Patricia fell and sustained a serious dislocation of her right shoulder, which caused recurring pain and required ongoing physical therapy. Again on February 2, 1990, on her way to lunch, Patricia slipped

HARRINGTON, PATRICIA
000-876-979-6
04-14-41

☐ Skilled Nursing Facility
☒ Outpatient Dept.

PROBLEM LIST SIGNIFICANT FOR PHYSICAL THERAPY REFERRAL: ONSET

#	1	Peroneal Nerve Palsy L side a) Unable to take shower independently	02/02/90
	2	L knee instability b) Unable to shop for 1/2 hr before resting	02/02/94
#	3	R shoulder pain and UE pain	03/18/94
		a) Decreased ROM R shoulder	
#		b) R shoulder pain prevents cooking 1 meal without having to rest	
		c) Unable to sleep through the night secondary to R shoulder pain (5 years approx)	
#			

PROGRESS: S: "While I was at my son's they helped me to lower down into the hot tub. I think I stayed in for too long because when I got out I felt light headed and I had to rest for quite some time. It was difficult for me to get back upstairs because my foot was swollen and I had to wait for the swelling to go out of my foot before I could put my brace on." O: Patient has been seen in physical therapy approx. 38 times including today since beginning her therapy on 02/08/94. PAIN: Patient has noted increased pain in R shoulder/neck area since her visit to the Carolina's which has been approx. 1 month since her last PT treatment session. Patient has noted increased low back pain which to date has not been ASSESSMENT addressed but at next treatment session will initiate low back eval.
MOBILITY: Patient's mobility has not improved since last PT treatment session approx. 1 month ago to date. Patient did ambulate on uneven surfaces, and sand well on vacation but the consistency was decreased compared to PT treatment sessions.
PROGRAM: Remains the same from last recertification of ambulation on various surfaces, GOAL (SHORT TERM) bike riding. Home program consisting of UE exercises.
ASSESSMENT: Patient's progress has been limited throughout the last month secondary to no PT intervention treatment. Feel that patient is continuing to benefit from PT treatment GOALS (LONG TERM) sessions, as this is seen with no progress made throughout the last month as patient was away on vacation. Feel that it is time to address patients low back pain as she has a good home program that's working on ambulating. Feel that by addressing low back pain and re-assessing neck pain will be able to hopefully decrease patients pain and increase functional ability. Discussed this plan with patient who feels that this is an appropriate time to work on these areas and start with this plan as well.
SHORT TERM GOALS REMAIN THE SAME FROM LAST RECERTIFICATION

P: 1) Continue functional activity program as much as possible increasing this at home.
MEDICARE/CAID ☐ Will initiate low back eval and re-assess shoulder pain starting at next
PHYSICIAN'S ADDITION AND COMMENTS: treatment session. Will continue to monitor goals and change as needed.

DATE OF FIRST TREATMENT   02/08/94

FREQUENCY: ☐ b.i.d. ☐ daily ☒ 2 x per week for 4 weeks   IF OUTPATIENT, PHYSICIAN WILL RE/EVALUATE ON____
RECERT. DATE 09/27/94
DATE SEEN BY PHYSICIAN: 06/24/94
THERAPIST SIGNATURE ____ R.P.T.
RECERTIFICATION SIGNATURE ____ M. D.

RECORD OF TREATMENTS

| MONTH/YEAR | TREATMENTS | 1 | 2 | 3 | 4 | 5 | 6 | 7 | 8 | 9 | 10 | 11 | 12 | 13 | 14 | 15 | 16 | 17 | 18 | 19 | 20 | 21 | 22 | 23 | 24 | 25 | 26 | 27 | 28 | 29 | 30 | 31 |

FORM 779-009 (5/78)

In this report from September 27, 1994, Patricia's physical therapist lists the three main problems she was having: peroneal nerve palsy, left knee instability and right shoulder pain. The therapist also notes Patricia's mobility had not improved during her care.

on a patch of solid ice and hyperextended her knee. As a result, she sustained a seriously pulled hamstring.

Just over two weeks after that fall, thinking she had recovered enough to venture into town, Patricia carefully braved the recently snow-plowed driveway to reach the car of a friend who had come to assist her. "As I neared the car," she related, "my left foot slipped and twisted on a rock-hard ice patch. I slid under the car and hit my left shin on the frame with such force that I could feel an indentation on my shin."

Patricia was rushed to the hospital by ambulance, examined, given some pain medication and released.

Several days later a friend who was an orthopedic nurse stopped by the Harrington's home for a visit. "The moment she walked in the house she asked, 'Pat, what is wrong with your leg?'"

"My leg had swollen considerably, and my friend arranged for me to be taken back to the hospital immediately," she recalled.

That's when the doctors discovered that Patricia had apparently damaged the left peroneal nerve which helps regulate the leg from the knee down to the foot. It caused her foot to noticeably hang down.

Doctors placed her left leg in a short leg cast to treat the peroneal nerve injury, and she was taken home. Within days, however, she began feeling something so unusual she could hardly describe it. "It was as if I was being pulled into something electrical," she said. "My nerves were jangling, and suddenly my entire body would begin to shake. Again and again, it felt like electrical impulses going up my leg all the way to my brain."

On August 1, 1990, Patricia's doctors conducted tests on the left peroneal nerve and surrounding motor fibers. The test report showed that the peroneal nerve was no longer conducting electrical signals to the muscles. This confirmed a diagnosis of complete left peroneal nerve palsy.

Patricia's physical condition continued to spiral downward for the next four years. She had problems executing the basic necessities of life. She was only able to shop for about a half hour before needing rest; she was unable to cook more than one meal without requiring more rest; and she was unable to shower independently. The burden on Allen and others who took care of her became enormous. Her sister, Carol, became Patricia's principal caregiver.

Patricia states, "I had muscle spasms throughout my body. My hamstrings were stretched like rubber bands from hyperextending my knee, and there was nothing left to hold me up." All the while her right shoulder continued to give her pain as well.

Patricia had been fitted with a heavy leather brace about ten inches wide that was held in place with a Velcro backing to give stability to her left knee and leg. Another brace supported her kneecap. Metal bars came down the sides of her calves into a special cushioned shoe to help ease the severe pain.

"My whole body was twisted to one side because of my constant attempts to balance myself," she said. "A special hydraulic chair lifted me since I could not stand without some kind of assistance."

Patricia's physical therapy report on September 27, 1994, stated three main problems: peroneal nerve palsy, left knee instability and right shoulder pain. By this time she had been seen by her physical therapist thirty-eight times and was scheduled to continue therapy.

"Tomorrow Night!"

When Patricia learned that we would be conducting a crusade in the fall of 1994 in Worcester, Massachusetts, she was overjoyed. "I had been hearing about your ministry, Pastor Benny, for several years and was determined that I was going to be at those meetings."

The work schedule of Patricia's husband would not permit him to attend, but Lydia Loiselle, a seventy-six-year-old friend who had been praying for her recovery, offered to drive her to the meetings. "From the moment I knew I was going to Worcester, my faith began to rise," Patricia stated. "One scripture stayed before me constantly:

> Being confident of this very thing, that he which hath begun a good work in you will perform it until the day of Jesus Christ (Phil. 1:6, KJV).

On Thursday evening, October 21, 1994, Patricia was wheeled into the vast arena by her elderly friend. "I was dizzy and nauseated as she pushed me to the wheelchair section," she recalled. "I wondered if I was going to make it through the service."

Patricia was greatly encouraged, however, when two members of our crusade staff, Kent Mattox and

Dave Palmquist, came to where she was seated and quietly prayed for her. They were led of the Lord to tell her, "Tomorrow night is your night!"

Later, in her motel room, the battle with pain continued. Before the service the next day she felt the Lord telling her to remove the two special devices attached to her back that sent electronic vibrations into her system in an attempt to diffuse the pain. "You are not going to be needing those," His voice said.

Patricia and Lydia arrived about four hours before the service. "Even in the midst of the pain, I never stopped praying and believing," she said. The moment the choir began rehearsing she began singing along, and suddenly her legs began to bounce to the sound of the music. Patricia said, "My body was beginning to stretch and straighten up. I raised my hands to heaven and realized my shoulder had been healed."

The Lord brought to her remembrance the scene of Peter stepping out of the boat and walking on the water toward Christ. Patricia stated, "The Lord was saying to me, 'Pat, step out of the boat, and I will meet you.'"

Somehow she managed to stand on her feet. "At that moment I felt my kneecap beginning to move around." She turned to her friend and said, "Would you help me take this brace off?"

Once the brace was under the chair she said, "Lydia, quick! Put your hand on my knee." Both of them felt changes taking place in her left knee. "It was awesome!" said Patricia.

"I put my hand on Pat's kneecap and literally felt

Harrington, Patricia   4/14/41   8769796

Date of Service: 10/26/94

Attending Physician: ██████ █. ████, █.█.
Referring Physician:

P: Bilateral knee pain, multiple musculoskeletal complaints.

S: This pt. comes in today stating that she is essentially pain
free except for some residual problems with her right lower
extremity which had a peroneal palsy although this has improved
and continues to improve She states that she has in fact been to
a faith healing session and with that has had a significant change
and improvement in her symptoms. According to the note of 5/11/94,
it is apparent that she has had significant problems included and
enumerated in the note of 2/2/94. Essentially these related to her
left knee instability which was symptomatic and complete peroneal
palsy and multiple functional impairments. In the past she has had
a number of other problems, such as a right shoulder dislocation.
She has been symptomatic, and although she has had some improvement
with PT, she really has been quite functionally impaired. Today
she is able to walk with a significantly more normal gait. She
denies any pain or discomfort in any areas except for the more mild
residual upper right peroneal palsy.

O: On exam she has essentially a normal gait today. She has good
ROM of her hips, knees, and ankles. Has some dorsiflexor power of
the right peroneal nerve function which on 3/9/94 she had no EHL
or TA.   .

A: It is my opinion that her exam and discussion today represented
significant change from the other times that I have seen her

██████ █. ████, █.█.
███/███

cc of this note, 2/2/94 note, and 3/9/94 note to the pt.

the Lord replace it! I could feel parts moving around inside like it was being reformed, and it began to feel solid. It was an amazing moment," said Lydia.

One of our staff members, noticing the commotion, came over and asked, "What is happening?"

"I'm being healed!" Patricia exclaimed.

Speechless in Worcester

At that point the pain was still present, but she felt her body become more sturdy. "I took a few halting steps and wobbled along, and I could feel myself getting stronger," she said.

As an act of faith, Patricia had brought a pair of shoes along with her, but now she couldn't find them. "Fortunately, Lydia had a pair of slippers in her large purse, and I put them on and continued to walk," she remembered.

During the service, a member of our team walked over to a smiling Patricia and said, "Come with me." They walked through the crowd to the steps leading to the platform. Patricia looked at those steps and said, "Lord, I'm going to trust You."

By the time she reached the last step the pain was completely gone, and she was speechless. "All I could do was sing," she recalled. At that moment, God's power touched her in an unusual way.

"It was much more than a momentary blessing," said Patricia. "I was totally healed and have never worn that brace again."

She could hardly wait to see her physician. "I'm here to submit myself to any test you deem necessary to prove this is a miracle," she told him.

HARRISON, PATRICIA

PROBLEM LIST SIGNIFICANT FOR PHYSICAL THERAPY REFERRAL:	ONSET
1) Peroneal Nerve Palsy L side a) Unable to take shower independently	02/02/90
# b) Unable to shop for ¼ hour before resting ---resolved 10-28-94	
# 2) L knee instability ----resolved 10-28-94	02-02-94
# 3) R shoulder pain and UE pain	03-18-94
a) decreased ROM R shoulder	
# b) R shoulder pain prevents cooking one meal without having to rest. --resolved 10-28-9	
c) Unable to sleep through the night secondary to R shoulder pain (5 years approx.)	

PROGRESS:

S: "You should have seen it. I was standing there and I was bouncing and bouncing and all of a sudden there just wasn't anymore pain and I felt like I could go on forever. I don't have anymore pain at this time. There is no pain in my foot, my back, shoulders, neck. You can touch my toe and there is no more sensetivity there. I can kick. I can do anything. I still have somewhat of a drop foot but ▓▓▓▓ thinks that will resolve as well."

O: Patient has been seen in PT 44 times including today since beginning her therapy on 2-08-94. PAIN: Patient states that there is no pain in R shoulder/neck area, as well as low ▓▓▓▓▓▓▓▓▓▓ back area or bilateral knee pain. Patient states that she has not had any pain since going to her religous healing festival in Mass. (MOBILITY:) At this time patient is not using her L LE brace and patient feels as though she can do anything. Patient is now able to rise from a low seated position which before this she was unable to do. Patient was able to get in and out of a bath tub in order to shower. Patient is able to do all the shopping, ▓▓▓▓▓▓▓▓▓▓▓▓▓ household chores and sleeping without any pain noted as well as cooking meals. At this time it appears that patient is able to perform and do any task that she wishes at this time without any limiting pain.

A: At this time patient seems to have been healed by a miracle as she has no pain at this ▓▓▓▓▓▓▓▓▓▓▓ time. Patient does note to have a slight foot drop on the L. But per patient her physician feels that this may resolve as well. Patient may wish to obtain an AFO it this is not clear but patient is still able to function independently without her L LE brace. At this time patient has achieved all short term/long term goals which have been decribed above. I feel that patient doesn't need any further PT intervention at this time ▓▓▓▓ and if a need arises at a later date patient is encouraged to return to PT to address these areas.

P: PROGRAM: Discontinue patient from PT. ADDITIONAL INFORMATION: N/A PATIENT EDUCATION: N/A
MEDICARE/CAID [ ] D/C PLAN: D/C patient from PT services

PHYSICIAN'S ADDITION AND COMMENTS:

DATE OF FIRST TREATMENT

FREQUENCY:	[ ] b.i.d.	[ ] daily	[ ] ___ x per week	IF OUTPATIENT, PHYSICIAN WILL
RECERT. DATE			for____weeks	RE-EVALUATE ON____
10-28-94				

DATE SEEN BY PHYSICIAN:	THERAPIST SIGNATURE ▓▓▓▓▓▓▓▓	R.P.T.
06-24-94	RECERTIFICATION SIGNATURE	M. D.

RECORD OF TREATMENTS

MONTH/YEAR	TREATMENTS	1	2	3	4	5	6	7	8	9	10	11	12	13	14	15	16	17	18	19	20	21	22	23	24	25	26	27	28	29	30	31
10/9?																																

64 779-009 (3/78)

Just six days after Patricia was restored by the Lord's healing touch, her physical therapist wrote, "resolved 10-28-94" next to Patricia's list of problems. She had mobility and no longer needed physical therapy.

"Patricia, I can see it is a miracle!" said the doctor.

After the doctor pounded on her knee and stretched her leg, the interns were called in to see this amazing turnaround.

Her physician wrote, "It is my opinion that her exam and discussion today represented significant change from the other times that I have seen her...On exam she has essentially a normal gait."

On October 28, 1994, one week after the crusade, Patricia's physical therapist wrote, "At this time the patient seems to have been healed by a miracle as she has no pain." Where the report had previously stated all of her problems (peroneal nerve palsy, left knee instability and right shoulder pain), it now read, "resolved — October 28, 1994."

"The therapist was so excited she videotaped me," Patricia recalled.

Today Patricia and Allen live in a small community near Burlington, Vermont, and minister to people everywhere. She recently stated, "It's been over a year and a half now, and the pain is totally gone. God has allowed me to walk once again. And one of these days I believe I will be able to run as I did when I was a child on that farm!"

Lessons From
the Great Physician

From there Jesus took a trip to Tyre and Sidon. They had hardly arrived when a Canaanite woman came down from the hills and pleaded, "Mercy, Master, Son of David! My daughter is cruelly afflicted by an evil spirit."

Jesus ignored her. The disciples came and complained, "Now she's bothering us. Would you please take care of her? She's driving us crazy."

Jesus refused, telling them, "I've got my hands full dealing with the lost sheep of Israel."

Then the woman came back to Jesus, went to her knees and begged. "Master, help me."

He said, "It's not right to take bread out of children's mouths and throw it to dogs."

She was quick: "You're right, Master, but beggar dogs do get scraps from the master's table."

Jesus gave in. "Oh, woman, your faith is something else. What you want is what you get!" Right then her daughter became well.

Matthew 15:21-28

Jesus gave in. "Oh woman, your faith is something else. What you want is what you get!" Right then her daughter became well.

10

Danny's Heavenly Pacemaker

DANNY WAS THE most beautiful baby I had ever seen," Those were the words of Elva Garcia when she first saw her adopted son Danny. At the time he was four days old and weighed about four pounds.

Without the aid of a nurse or doctor, Elva's sister-in-law had given birth to the baby boy in her small home in Diaz Ordaz, Tamaulipas, Mexico, across the Rio Grande River from South Texas. Elva felt a connection to that tiny baby the first time she laid eyes on him. "A love had entered my heart as that of a mother for her own child, and I could not understand what God's plan was, but I knew that this baby was part of my life."

Several weeks passed and Elva and her husband drove from their home in Roma, Texas, to visit the baby and his mother again. Only this time they discovered a thin baby who had not been eating. She asked her sister-in-law to let her bring him back to the United States to get him some help, but the woman was afraid and said no. Elva returned home in fervent prayer for this tiny baby as he teetered on the threshold of life.

"He would not eat, and he was growing worse each time I went to Mexico to see him. At last it was getting so bad I stopped going to visit because my heart was breaking for this baby, and I was not allowed to do anything for him," she remembered.

Finally she received a call from the baby's grandfather telling her that if she still wanted the baby she could come and get him. When she arrived in Mexico, the dark-haired child was being given oxygen and digitalis (a cardiac stimulant drug) for a heart condition. Pneumonia had attacked his fragile body, and doctors had given him only three days to live. He was one year and three months old, yet he weighed less than nine pounds.

"He's beautiful," Elva told the baby's mother. "We would love to adopt him." She promised that she and her husband would do their best to nurse the child back to health.

Not knowing whether the child would live or die, they lovingly accepted the baby and drove him to their home. He was given the name Eduardo "Danny" Garcia.

"His condition was so weak he could not take a bottle.

122

PATIENT: Garcia, Eduardo Daniel   **CLINIC:**
BIRTH DATE: 11-27-78   **TOWN:**
PRESENT DATE: 1-29-92

<u>SUBJECTIVE:</u>
13 year 2 month old male with history of Post Operative Ventricular Septal
Defect with Pacemaker. Returns doing well.

<u>OBJECTIVE:</u>
PHYSICAL EXAMINATION: WT; 73 lbs. HT; 57 1/2 in. HC: n/a. CC: n/a. HR; 70.
RR: 20. BP-RA: 102/60. LA; n/a. RL; n/a. LL: n/a.
GENERAL APPEARANCE: Well nourished, no distress.
BEHAVIOR: Cooperative, Calm.
HEENT: Normal.
NECK: Negative.
CHEST: Symmetrical.
LUNGS: Clear.
SKIN: n/a.
HEART: No thrills present. Peripheral pulses are equal and strong. Apex
impulse is at the 5th left intercostal space along the midclavicular line.
No right ventricle impulse present. Harsh systolic ejection murmur grade
I/VI at left lower sternal border. No diastolic murmur present. First heart
sound is split. Second heart sound is normal, No ejection click present.
ABDOMEN: Negative.
EXTREMITIES: Negative.
CHEST X-RAY: n/a.
EKG: Normal 100% Pacemaker.
TWO DIMENSIONAL ECHO: n/a.
M MODE ECHO: n/a.

<u>ASSESSMENT:</u>
DIAGNOSIS: (1) Post Operative Ventricular Septal Defect.
(2) Post Operative DDD Pacemaker.

<u>PLAN:</u>
DIAGNOSTIC: (1) Return to clinic in 2 months with EKG.
(2) Continue Precautions Against Subacute Bacterial Endocarditis with
Routine Dental Care. (3) Moderate restrictions.
(4) Call Corpus and get pacemaker check.

_____
Medical Director

cc:

**This EKG note from a routine checkup on
January 29, 1992, shows that Danny's heartbeat was normal,
but completely regulated by the pacemaker.**

We had to feed him with an eye dropper," remembered Elva. "The doctors were not encouraging. It was obvious they considered his case hopeless."

Perhaps the most important lifeline for Danny was the love he was receiving from his new parents and the watchful eye of his Maker.

Clinging to Life

The Garcias arranged for X-rays to be taken of the child, and it was determined that his heart was extremely enlarged. Other tests confirmed that he had a chronic congenital heart defect.

"Danny's first heart surgery was at the tender age of one year and seven months," Elva recounted. "His life was in jeopardy from the operation because of the malnutrition he had suffered during the first months of his life. They patched a hole in his heart, but his weak muscles could barely hold the stitches. He was given practically zero chance of survival."

Somehow the baby clung to life.

"We didn't try to compare Danny with other children," his mother told me. "We only knew how far he had come from that day when we brought him home from Mexico."

Physicians who were monitoring Danny's progress recommended that he travel to a major hospital in Houston, Texas, for open-heart surgery on November 24, 1982, three days before his fourth birthday. The hole that had been patched in the first surgery had come undone, therefore requiring the second surgery. During the operation, doctors noticed that Danny's heart was not beating properly on its own, so they installed temporary pacing wires to control the heart-beat.

In the following thirteen days Danny underwent a series of tests to see if he needed a permanent pace-maker. The tests revealed two problems with his heart: the triggering mechanism that acts as a natural pacemaker to make his heart beat wasn't working properly; and there was a blockage between that trig-gering mechanism and the pumping chambers of his heart. The blockage would make it difficult for the electrical impulses to reach the pumping chambers of his heart that pumped the blood. At this point doctors decided Danny needed the permanent pacemaker.

"Danny has an irregular heartbeat, and it does not want to beat fast enough on its own. It needs help," the doctors counseled Elva. On December 7, 1984, Danny had a permanent pacemaker installed near his stomach.

"Every time I wore a belt it was really uncomfort-able," the young man stated.

Danny could sense that something unnatural was reg-ulating his system. "The pacemaker was set at a fixed rate of eighty beats per minute, but I was too hyper for that, and it tried to slow me down. It was weird," said Danny.

At night, he had the opposite reaction. "I had a dif-ficult time falling asleep," he remembered. "My heart wanted to slow down, but those eighty beats per minute kept pounding away."

At the supper table one evening when he was seven, Danny complained, "I really don't feel very well." He felt something happening inside that was different.

He went to bed early that night. Sleep would not come, and before long he was calling to his mother, "I think it's my heart."

Immediately, she checked his pulse and his pacemaker. "They told me this gadget was designed to last at least ten years, but I think it's going dead," she said in distress. "Quick, son, we've got to get you to the hospital in Houston."

"I'll never forget that ride! Mom must have thought she was driving an ambulance," Danny recalled. "She was weaving in and out of traffic, rushing me to the emergency room." The results? Another operation. Another pacemaker. This time doctors put the pacemaker in his left chest.

What was it like to enter public school with such a severe medical problem? "It did not take me long to realize that I was not exactly like other kids," Danny recalled. "I could never stick quarters in the candy machine or drink anything with caffeine in it. I had to avoid anything that raised a normal person's heart rate, including playing sports at recess."

Sports were off limits. The doctors didn't want him to stimulate his heartbeat, and they were also worried that he might be bumped during play. Contained in his file is a letter by his physician to school officials. The doctor wrote, "Danny has a congenital heart condition with a pacemaker. Danny should not participate in physical education courses — *ever.*

What was the lifetime prognosis for Danny? He would hardly be able to function without the heart regulator. He would never be able to engage in strenuous activities because his heart couldn't reliably beat fast enough to keep up. And his condition would need to be regularly monitored. It was a daunting future for a boy who was about to become a teenager.

"I Just Know It!"

The Garcias attended a Bible-believing, faith-inspiring church in their small community of Roma. They believed in miracles even before Elva began watching our daily telecast. For many years, she had told her son, "One of these days, I know the Lord is going to allow you to live without that pacemaker."

When it was announced that our crusade team was coming to Houston in January 1993, a large group from the family's church made plans to attend.

Elva couldn't afford to make the trip at the time and decided not to go. But one morning the Lord told her, "If you take Danny to Houston, I will heal him." Elva rejoiced at that word. She heard the Lord say this to her a second time but asked Him to confirm it. She waited all day thinking surely someone would tell her to take Danny to Houston. By the time she had arrived home that evening, no one had said anything to confirm what she'd heard.

"I was cleaning in the kitchen and praying and told God that since He had not confirmed His word to me I must have been mistaken," Elva recalled. "About that time Danny came into the house shouting, 'Mom, Mom, you've got to take me to Houston, because if you take me, God is going to heal me.' That was my confirmation! God had given it to Danny himself," Elva recounted.

Fourteen-year-old Danny and his mother made the trip. On the journey, Elva repeated again and again, "Son, I know you are going to be healed. I just know it!"

On Thursday evening, January 14, 1993, the opening night of the crusade, there was a mighty move of God in the service. The platform was lined with people who received their healing. "I prayed I would be in that number," said Danny, "yet nothing seemed to happen."

The following night, however, the young man felt something stirring within him from the time he and his friends found their seats far in the back of the large auditorium. "As soon as the service began, something inside me was saying, 'This is your day!'" he recalled.

Danny will never forget the words God inspired me to say from the platform that evening. As he told me, "Pastor Benny, you looked in my direction and said, 'There's a young man sitting in front of me who was just healed of a heart condition.'"

The moment he heard those words Danny knew they were meant for him. "It was as if electricity hit me and began flowing through my body," he recalled. "I was not frightened by it. I felt warm and alive."

Elva knew it, too. "When the power of God hit Danny he began jumping up and down. I was sitting in front of him and quickly turned around and tried to grab his legs to steady him." She also described something else that happened. "Many of those immediately around him were knocked to the floor, including several people who were there from our church."

Danny did not share his testimony on the platform, but he knew a miracle had touched his heart.

It Was Real

"In the car on our way home that night I knew something was different," said Danny. "When I was small I could never feel my heart, only the pacemaker beating for me. That night, however, what was beating inside me was not artificial, it was my real heart."

His mother was rejoicing. "We are going to let God show the doctors that you are healed," she told him. They decided not even to talk to the doctors about what happened.

"I told God that He had worked this wonderful miracle, and I wasn't going to interfere, that I was going to let Him do the whole thing," Elva said. They waited and prayed and prayed. Danny just continued to get better. He started growing rapidly and began to eat much better than he ever had before. Danny grew strong, and his studies improved, but Elva said, "God still didn't act."

Finally, on July 9, 1993, his pacemaker began emitting strange vibrations, and he tried to describe the sensation to his mother. "I think we need to have this checked out," he told her.

Elva sent an EKG over the phone and the person on duty at the hospital told her to take Danny to a nearby hospital right away because the pacemaker was not working right. Elva continued to monitor Danny and finally took him to the hospital in Corpus Christi, against the doctors wishes because of the distance. But she knew Danny would be fine. It was midnight when they arrived.

"They examined him until about four in the morning

129

and could not figure out what was happening," his mother related. Then one of the surgeons said, "We're going to operate at ten o'clock in the morning and put in a new pacemaker."

During those early morning hours, Elva prayed that somehow the doctors would realize that a miracle had occurred and that surgery wasn't necessary.

Danny was in intensive care when the physicians came into his room to explain what they were about to do. "The new pacemaker you will receive is very tiny and much better than the one you have now," they told him.

Danny suddenly became frightened, and the blips on the video monitor began rapidly increasing, faster and faster. The doctors called others around and said, "Look! His heart can't do that!" For ten long years, Danny's heart had required the pacemaker just so it would beat fast enough for him to be alert and function. Now his heart was exceeding the rate the pacemaker had maintained.

"Danny, we want you to calm down," the doctors told him.

Immediately they gave him a series of tests. First he was asked to walk in place and then run in place. The monitor did not lie. His heart began beating more rapidly, up to 172 beats a minute. Then they asked him to lie down and the rate returned to about eighty beats. When he ran once more it again increased to 172. The doctors were in disbelief. "We are going to postpone the operation. It seems as if Danny's heart is beating adequately on its own," they announced.

Danny was released from the hospital on July 13,

PATIENT: Garcia, Eduardo   DOB: 11/27/78

LOCATION: HOSP MR#: ▓▓▓▓▓   DATE: ADM 7/24/93
                                                DIS 7/30/93

DOCTOR: ▓▓▓▓▓▓▓, ▓.▓.

DISCHARGE SUMMARY

CHIEF COMPLAINT: This is a 14 year old male with a history of VSD repair at the age of 1 year and 7 month. The patient had a pacemaker placed on 10/24/85 (7005 model, serial #GN20085294). He was recently discharged from DCH for pacemaker malfunction. The patient was sent home with a Holter monitor, and admitted at this time for Holter monitoring for 48 hours to decide about removing the pacemaker. He has been asymptomatic.

Past Medical History: Remarkable for bronchitis in January; treated with antibiotics. Surgical history is remarkable for surgery in the past and placement of pacemaker in 1985. Immunizations are up to date. Pre-natal and post-natal are unknown as the patient is adopted. Apparently delivery was at home and was spontaneous vaginal. Birth weight was 4 lb. Development is adequate for age.

Social History: Four siblings at home. Some history of TB in the family. Otherwise, there is no other information available on the family history. The patient lives with his adoptive mother. ▓▓▓▓▓▓▓▓▓▓▓▓▓▓▓▓ ▓▓▓▓▓▓▓▓▓▓▓▓▓▓▓▓▓▓. No one smokes.

PHYSICAL: Temperature 97.2 F, pulse 76, respiratory rate 20, blood pressure 105/61, weight 41.3 kg, height 156 cm. The patient was awake, alert and in no acute distress. HEENT were normal. Neck - supple; no adenopathy. Chest - asymmetric; evidence of pacemaker placement in left anterior chest wall subcutaneously. Lungs - clear bilaterally. CVS - rhythmic; heart sounds normal; no murmurs. Abdomen - flat; no hepatosplenomegaly; bowel sounds present. ▓▓▓▓▓▓▓▓▓▓▓▓▓▓▓▓ Skin - normal. Extremities - good capillary refill; good peripheral pulses in all four extremities; DTR's present. CNS - awake, cooperative and oriented; no focal deficits.

HOSPITAL COURSE: The patient was admitted for 48 hours of Holter monitoring. The monitoring showed sinus rhythm, for which reason the decision to remove the pacemaker was made.

TREATMENT/PROGRESS: ▓▓ ▓▓▓▓ had the pacemaker removed on 7/29/93, with no complications. Holter monitoring was repeated after the pacemaker was removed, which also showed sinus rhythm.

This report from July 30, 1993, shows that after Danny's pacemaker was removed, his heart was beating normally (which is called sinus rhythm). Danny had worn his pacemaker since he was three-and-a-half years old.

PATIENT: Garcia, Edwardo   DOB: 11-27-78

LOCATION: HOSP#: ▓▓▓▓   DATE: ADM: 7-9-93
                                                     DIS: 7-13-93
DOCTOR;   ▓▓▓▓

DISCHARGE SUMMARY

This is a 14 year ˜ month old known cardiac patient with history of VSD
repair at one year 7 months and at 4 years of age. Had a left pulmonary
artery correction. Initially had a VSD repair at one year 7 months and then
had a left pulmonary artery and aortic valve lavage after 2 years after
surgical procedure. Also a pacemaker was implanted and revised in 1985.
Mother noticed two days ago that the patient became sleepy and tired. Mother
checked pulse and showed pulse irregularities. Mother found that the
pacemaker battery was not functioning. Patient came for medical attention.
The patient lives in Roma, Texas.   The pacemaker implanted 10-24-85 is ˜005
Model. Serial # TN2008S294. No medications.

PAST MEDICAL HISTORY: This is an adopted child. He has VSD as mentioned
previously. No left pulmonary artery. Heart surgery was done at ▓▓▓▓
▓▓▓▓▓▓▓▓▓▓▓▓▓▓▓▓▓▓▓▓▓▓▓ and other problems because of heart condition.
              IMMUNIZATIONS ARE APPARENTLY UP TO DATE.

DEVELOPMENT: Adequate for age.

SOCIAL: Lives with adopted mother, alone.   There is no family history
available due to the patient being adopted.

PHYSICAL EXAM: On admission temp 9˜.9, weight 41.1 kg, height 152 cm, RR
128, pulse 168. BP 115/69 in left arm, 115/61 in right arm.   General
condition - alert, no acute distress.   Physical exam in general
unremarkable, except for low heart rate. Otherwise completely within normal
limits. The patient had an initial impression of pacemaker malfunction, had
an EKG, chest x-ray, urinalysis, CBC, electrolytes and type and cross.

The patient was admitted to ICU for close observation. Due to his remarkable
improvement, he was transferred to the floor the second day of
hospitalization.   Also the pacemaker was revised and the patient had a
Holter monitor placed the day of the hospitalization which showed some low
heart rate consistent with heart block. Also had a treadmill stress test
which seemed like   heart responded remarkably well, not within normal
limits but went up to 172 after excercise. Second Holter monitor after the
stress test continued to show some slowing of the heart rate 39 when
sleeping for which reason the patient otherwise remained stable on the
floor. The patient on 7-13-93 after review of the Holter monitor and check
with cardiologist in Houston, was decided to be discharged home on no
medications, to have a recheck of the Holter monitor in a week. Have follow
up with ▓▓▓▓   in a week and to decide removing of the pacemaker after
reviewing the Holter in a week.

**The doctor's notes dated July 13, 1993, from Danny's hospital
visit (due to a pacemaker malfunction) after he was touched so
miraculously by God, show "remarkable improvement."**

1993. His doctors gave him a holter monitor to wear that would record the activity of his heart. The doctors, reluctant to remove the pacemaker until more tests were done, said, "We've turned off the pacemaker, but since there is a little bit of juice left in it, we have decided to leave it in him for now just in case his heart goes into a lock and it needs to be turned back on."

Finally, on July 29, 1993, they removed the pacemaker because his heart was in "sinus rhythm." In other words, his heart was beating just as a normal person's heart beats.

A New Report

Danny has been examined many times since. During one stress test in August 1995, he ran for a record sixteen minutes with no sign of a problem. He laughs when he thinks about the doctor who told school officials he could not be involved in physical education "ever."

At school, he signed up for Olympic wrestling and won seven out of eight bouts, losing only to a football player. "Now I'm playing tennis, eating chocolate and doing all the fun things I missed for most of my life," he said. He most recently decided to try out for his school's track team.

To Danny, who was once given little chance for survival by doctors, the medical words "monitoring showed sinus rhythm" simply mean, "Healed by the Great Physician."

Lessons From the Great Physician

As Jesus left the house, he was followed by two blind men crying out, "Mercy, Son of David! Mercy on us!" When Jesus got home, the blind men went in with him. Jesus said to them, "Do you really believe I can do this?" They said, "Why, yes, Master!"

He touched their eyes and said, "Become what you believe." It happened. They saw. Then Jesus became very stern. "Don't let a soul know how this happened." But they were hardly out the door before they started blabbing to everyone they met.

Right after that, as the blind men were leaving, a man who had been struck speechless by an evil spirit was brought to Jesus. As soon as Jesus threw the evil tormenting spirit out, the man talked away just as if he'd been talking all his life. The people were up on their feet applauding: "There's never been anything like this in Israel!"

The Pharisees were left sputtering, "Hocus pocus. It's nothing but hocus pocus. He's probably made a pact with the Devil."

Matthew 9:27-34

He touched their eyes and said,
**"Become what you believe." It happened.
They saw.**

11

On the
Road Again

ALAN AND SUZANNE Frick, a husband and wife truck driving team, were bobtailing down the road between Seattle, Washington, and Portland, Oregon on October 23, 1993. *Bobtailing* is trucker talk for driving the cab of a truck with no trailer in tow.

Suzanne was asleep in the bunk of the truck, and Alan was at the wheel when suddenly the cab, which didn't have air-ride suspension, unexpectedly hit a large chuckhole in the road. "I literally went flying up in the air and came down hard on my back," said Suzanne.

At first she felt a small sharp pain, but tried to brush it off as unimportant. The next day, however, the terrible ache persisted and became worse. "Earlier in my life I experienced kidney infections, and I thought perhaps the jolt had triggered something similar again," she recalled.

About five days later, after delivering two or three more loads for the trucking firm who employed them, Suzanne could hardly move. "I think I need to have this checked out," she told her husband as they were heading toward the state of Illinois.

When they reached the company terminal in Chicago, the manager arranged for her to see a doctor. "When the physician examined my back it was so sensitive I could hardly stand it," said Suzanne. Their company took them off the road, and she was ordered to have at least two days of complete bed rest at a local hotel. That night, as soon as she laid down, she felt her back, "lock up." She remembered it well. "Nothing like this had ever happened to me before, and I was frightened."

Early the next morning, after catching only a few minutes of sleep, she tried to get out of bed, but to her dismay her legs wouldn't respond. Alan immediately called for an ambulance, and Suzanne was rushed to a nearby hospital.

"The doctors gave me several injections, including one with cortisone, but that did not help," she said. Since Suzanne could not walk without assistance, they gave her a walker and a wheelchair.

Six days later on November 4, 1993, Suzanne was discharged from the hospital. When the doctors felt she could cope with her condition, Suzanne and Alan flew back to their home in Deming, New Mexico. The next day, she was able to see her own doctor who quickly made arrangements for her to be examined by a local orthopedic specialist. "He did not have an answer for the extreme pain I was experiencing so I was sent to a major clinic in El Paso, Texas," said Suzanne. She was admitted to a hospital and during the month of November 1993 was given extensive tests for her condition.

"I was in such severe pain, taking all kinds of medication," she recalled.

A Desperate Search

Suzanne received a working diagnosis of a disk injury in her low back. She was given a spinal injection with cortisone (to relieve the pain). "The injection alleviated the pain for a short time, but my condition continued to worsen," she recalled. The only two things that seemed to take her mind off the pain were gospel music on the radio and Christian television programs she watched on TBN.

Suzanne had been raised in a Jehovah Witness family in Indiana, and the events of her life had not been kind. She married and had three children who all ran away from home as teenagers in 1985. Three years later her husband died of a massive heart attack. "I blamed God for everything that had happened and could see myself heading for the trash heap of life."

Living alone and desperately poor in Prescott, Arizona, Suzanne did not know where to turn. "Suddenly, I heard a voice inside me say again and again, 'Go home, My child.'"

At the age of forty, a physical wreck from the life she had been leading, she took her few belongings and went to Deming, New Mexico, where her mother lived.

"You can stay with me under one condition," said her mom. "You have to go to church with me at least once a week." Her mother had left the Jehovah Witnesses after becoming a born-again Christian and finding God's truth in a Spirit-filled church.

The following day, Suzanne and her mother attended a small Assemblies of God church. "I sat as far in the back as I could, but the power of God pulled me to the altar where I found Jesus," she said. "The next night I went back — and the next. I couldn't stay away. Every time the church doors were opened, my mom and I were there."

Suzanne was saved one week, received the baptism of the Holy Spirit the next and a few days later was baptized in water.

In 1991, while she was working as a waitress in a popular truck stop, Alan Frick walked in one night and sat at her table. Five and a half hours later, they were still talking. "I knew the first time I met him that he was the man God had prepared for my life," recalled Suzanne. Six months later they were married in the little church they both attended.

Not wanting to be separated from her husband, Suzanne passed her exams as an over-the-road driver of those big eighteen-wheelers. They were hired as a husband/wife team by a freight company.

Now that her back condition had become the focus

NAME: FRICK, SUZANNE

DATE: March 30, 1995

CHIEF COMPLAINT: Back pain and leg pain.

HISTORY OF PRESENT ILLNESS: This 44 year old female, who works with her husband as a cross country truck driver, states that she was injured in October of 1993. While sleeping in the back of the truck, apparently the truck went over some bumps and jolted her up and down. The following morning on getting out of the bunk, she had a twinge of pain in her back. She had previously had a kidney infection, and thought perhaps this was it. As she continued to travel with the truck, she developed further progressive, severe pain. She states that when they arrived in Chicago she was having extreme pain in the low back area and had lost sensation in her legs. She was seen and evaluated by a physician there and told to get bed rest in a hotel, for a two day period of time. She subsequently got worse and was admitted to a hospital. She was treated non-surgically there. She did have evaluations, apparently with a MRI and she thinks also an EMG study.

She continued with pain and subsequently was sent home to Deming, NM, by air. She had continued symptomatology in her back, at that time, saw local physicians in Deming and was referred to a spinal surgeon in El Paso, TX.

She was seen, evaluated and treated further in El Paso with an epidural steroid block. This gave some relief for about four or five months, but she has again developed pain and sciatica in both legs, particularly severe in the right.

Symptoms of back and leg pain have been intermittent in severity since the injury, despite all treatment and many episodes of being incapacitated with back and leg pain.

Approximately three or four weeks ago her symptoms got worse and with her exacerbation of symptoms her complaints are one of low back pain with radiation down the back of both legs to the toes, more so on the right. Pain is worse with exertion and it is eased somewhat by using a TENS unit and with rest, but not completely so.

Suzanne's doctor describes her condition in
this report dated March 30, 1995.

of their lives, Alan resigned from the trucking firm and devoted his time to her care. Suzanne was able to leave the hospital and return home, but her condition remained extremely painful — not only in her back, but also in her legs.

"I had to use my walker constantly because after only a few steps my feet literally would give out on me," she said. "It's frightening when you lose the sensation of feeling in your legs. Time after time I fell and Alan would have to pull me up."

She was fitted with a TENS unit — a battery-operated pack she wore twenty-four hours a day that numbed her lower back with low-level electrical impulses.

In a year and a half, the trucking company paid over sixty-eight thousand dollars in medical bills. Financially, Suzanne and Alan existed on Suzanne's workmen's compensation checks.

Hanging on to Survival

In January 1995, the Holy Spirit spoke to Suzanne and said, "I want you to step out in faith. I want you to support the ministries that have blessed your life."

She began to watch our program, *This Is Your Day!*, every chance she could. "I was being fed spiritually by the program, and the Lord told me to become a covenant partner with the ministry," said Suzanne. "I knew I would be healed. It was only a matter of time."

Alan had accepted a position working for a wonderful Christian man who directed a mining operation just south of Deming. He came home one day and

Suzanne exclaimed, "I just heard on Benny Hinn's program that he is going to have a crusade in Oklahoma City in May. Alan, I don't know how possible it is, but we just have to be there."

Suzanne's situation was bleak. "My face looked as if it had been pumped full of air because of the heavy doses of medication I was taking. I was beyond pain, merely hanging on for survival," she said. Plus, she had developed an intense bitterness against the trucking company, holding them responsible for her problems. For long-term financial reasons, they were trying to say she had this ailment before she began working for them — which Suzanne knew was not true.

A week before the Oklahoma City crusade, there was a flurry of legal action in an attempt by the trucking company to settle the issues surrounding her case. Then Suzanne had a phone call from her husband's boss with a message she did not expect. "You are not going to receive your healing until you forgive and forget the trucking company."

That's exactly what she did. "When I released my bitterness, it was as if a hundred pounds of pressure was lifted from my shoulders. I knew that God was getting ready to do something great for me."

The trucking company demanded one final medical opinion, and the results were revealed that same week. The new doctor confirmed her low back and leg pain but also found additional abnormalities suggesting a more serious systemic illness. All he could do was request further medical studies.

Suzanne will never forget the physician's words,

ORTHOPAEDIC SURGERY   DISORDERS OF THE SPINE

Date: April 26, 1994   Insurance Co:

        Re: FRICK, Susan
        Emp:
        DOI: 10/29/93
        SSN:
        Claim #:
        Patient #:

DISABILITY RATING

DIAGNOSIS: Degenerative disc disease, L4 and L5.
           Herniated nucleus pulposus, L4.

I believe Ms. Frick has reached maximum medical improvement at this
time. Range of motion measurements were obtained in the office
which reveal 32 degrees of flexion, 0 degrees of extension, 12
degrees right lateral flexion, and 13 degrees left lateral flexion.
Sacral range of motion is 30 degrees of flexion and 6 degrees of
extension. Straight leg raising is measured at 33 degrees on the
right and 43 degrees on the left.

Based on The AMA Guides to Evaluation of Permanent Impairment the
patient carries a total body partial permanent impairment of 24%.
The range of motion measurements are valid according to The AMA
Guides to Evaluation of Permanent Impairment.

Ms. Frick will return to this office on an as needed basis only.

Enclosure

In a letter dated April 26, 1994, to her insurance company, one
of Suzanne's doctors describes her range of motion abilities.
Based on his findings, the doctor gave Suzanne a partial
permanent impairment rating.

"We can monitor you and try to keep the pain away as much as possible, but there is nothing more we can do."

She said, "My prayer during this time was, 'Lord, I will praise You until the day I die no matter what has happened. Even if I die in this condition, I will praise You!'"

Satan's Whispers

The Fricks left for Oklahoma City with Suzanne stretched out on a special bed Alan had made in the space behind the front seat of their pickup truck. Nevertheless, the trip was almost more than Suzanne could handle. She could not halt the tears that were flowing because of the unrelenting pain. "Have we done the wrong thing?" questioned Alan. "Should we turn back?"

"No. We have to be in those meetings," Suzanne answered with great determination.

During the trip she reached for her pain pills, only to discover they had vanished. "I clearly remember packing them," said Suzanne, "but now they were gone." She wondered, "Was the Lord trying to tell me something?"

Just as the woman in the New Testament with the issue of blood exercised her faith by stretching forth her hand to touch the hem of Christ's garment, Suzanne demonstrated her belief through the very act of taking this difficult journey.

After checking into a motel they joined Alan's boss and his wife, who had also come for the meetings. They arrived at the Myriad Convention Center several hours before the Thursday night meeting, May 11, 1995.

"Each step I took became more agonizing than the last," remembered Suzanne, determined to be in the services without using a wheelchair. "Satan was whispering to me, 'What is going to happen when you don't get your healing? What will you do then?'"

Because of her obviously desperate condition, the ushers led Suzanne toward a special section reserved for those who were either crippled or who needed special attention. When she saw her friends seated in a higher section, however, she turned to Alan and said, "Somehow I've got to get up there to be with them."

With her legs about to collapse beneath her, and crying with every step, Suzanne made the climb. People were watching every torturous move as Alan helped her along.

Then, when Suzanne looked down at the area they had left, she noticed a woman who was part of our ministry team praying for various people. "It seemed that each person she touched suddenly had the glow of a light surrounding them," she recalled. "Alan, I know I asked you to help me up here, but I've just got to go back and have her pray for me."

With every painful step back she heard a voice inside repeating the simple words, "Pray and believe, and you will receive."

It was still two hours before the service began when she reached her original location. The woman had just finished praying for a small child when Suzanne spoke to her and said, "The Lord sent me down here saying that if I prayed and believed with you, I would receive."

For the next fifteen minutes she prayed earnestly for Suzanne, who was now seated. "She held both of my hands and called on God with unbelievable power and authority."

Suddenly, something happened. "I felt a wave of burning heat flow through my back, and I heard God's voice telling me, 'Get up and walk!'"

Suzanne obeyed the Lord and took one step, then two. "Alan took my cane away, and I felt like a baby learning to walk."

The same voice returned, this time saying, "You've received it, My child. Now begin to run!"

As Suzanne described it, "Not only did I begin to run, but I had no more pain. It was gone!" People all around her began to clap their hands and praise the Lord. "I could hear a heavenly chorus of 'Glory to God in the highest!'" she exclaimed.

During the service Suzanne walked to the platform to give her testimony, and she has never stopped praising the Lord.

Suzanne's Surprises

When she returned to her doctor, he looked at her with great surprise, "You're not the same woman I've been treating. I can see you have changed, but I'm still going to give you a 10 percent disability," he commented, trying to protect her workmen's compensation benefits.

Suzanne told him, "I don't need it. I'm healed!"

After a thorough examination he released her from

FRICK, SUZANNE L.   ███-████
June 5, 1995

Patient returns, she is painfree. She states that she saw a
healing minister in Oklahoma and she has not had pain since. She
was alert and cheerful today, and moved with positive agility and
a smile.

Her HLA-B27 test remained positive and she was informed of this.

Physical examination today demonstrated negative straight leg
raising bilaterally. She remained with a diminished ankle jerk on
the right and some weakness of dorsiflexion of the right foot.

IMPRESSION: Herniated nucleus pulposus, L-5, S-1, treated non-
surgically, resolved and doing very well.

RECOMMENDATIONS: No further aggressive treatment needed. No
surgical indications present. Patient is functioning quite well,
but she does have residuals that are compatible with a herniated
nucleus pulposus, and compatible with a radiculopathy being
present.   In reviewing the AMA Guide for Permanent Physical
Impairment, 4th Edition, her findings fit her into a Diagnosis
Related Estimate lumbosacral Category III, which states that this
equates to a 10% whole person impairment.   ███ ██
LETTER

**This doctor's note from June 5, 1995, three-and-a-half weeks
after the crusade, describes Suzanne's condition after the Lord
restored her. Essentially the report says that she could raise her
legs to a 90-degree angle while laying on her back.**

his care. On the official record of that final June 5, 1995, visit he wrote, "Patient returns. She is pain free. She was alert and cheerful today and moved with positive agility and a smile."

The only remaining symptom from her ordeal was a slight weakness in her right foot and ankle.

One of Suzanne's greatest joys was a trip to Arkansas where she visited the headquarters of the trucking company for which they had both worked. "I not only proclaimed how God had performed a miracle, but I demonstrated it — running, bending over and jumping all around their offices!"

Within a few days, the trucking company called and asked her to appear in an Oklahoma City claims court to settle the case. "They wrote out a substantial check and were thrilled that I would be off their records forever," Suzanne smiled.

Two separate judges called her aside and said, "Do you realize what you are giving up? Are you sure this is what you want?"

"Yes," she said, "I have been healed, and I want to be totally released from this."

Their first act after receiving the funds was to pay tithes on their unexpected income.

On Mother's Day, 1995, Suzanne was in for her ultimate surprise. "Mother, is that you?" said the voice on the line. It was one of her twin sons, living in Michigan, whom she had not heard from in years. "Mom, you didn't do anything wrong. We just wanted to go out and conquer the world. We love you."

Suzanne could not stop the tears of joy. Soon she was wonderfully reunited with all three of her children.

THIS IS YOUR DAY FOR A MIRACLE

The Lord also opened the doors for Alan and Suzanne to work again as a husband and wife trucking team. "Our first load was to take thirty-three thousand pounds of cookies to Vacaville, California — and there was no one there to do the unloading," she said. "It took us six hours to move those boxes, but God showed me that night that when He heals, He does a complete job."

Declared Suzanne, "He has restored my health, my family and has given me more than I ever deserved. I tell everyone that my turn-around began when I made the decision to become a covenant partner with this ministry. I sincerely believe that if I had rejected what God told us to do, I would not have received what He was waiting to give."

Alan and Suzanne are on the road again. "We are praising the Lord with every mile — even the bumps along the way."

Lessons From the Great Physician

There was a woman...so twisted and bent over with arthritis that she couldn't even look up. She had been afflicted with this for eighteen years. When Jesus saw her, he called her over. "Woman, you're free!" He laid hands on her and suddenly she was standing straight and tall, giving glory to God.

The meeting-place president, furious because Jesus had healed on the Sabbath, said to the congregation, "Six days have been defined as work days. Come on one of the six if you want to be healed, but not on the seventh, the Sabbath."

But Jesus shot back, "You frauds! Each Sabbath every one of you regularly unties your cow or donkey from its stall, leads it out for water, and thinks nothing of it. So why isn't it all right for me to untie this daughter of Abraham and lead her from the stall where Satan has had her tied these eighteen years?"

When he put it that way, his critics were left looking quite silly and red-faced. The congregation was delighted and cheered him on.

Luke 13:11-17

Jesus shot back, "...Why isn't it all right for me to untie this daughter of Abraham and lead her from the stall where Satan has had her tied these eighteen years?"

12

"A Resurrection From the Living Dead"

*By faith some women received back their
dead, raised to life again (Heb. 11:35).*

T HERE ARE SOME things worse than being
dead," a distraught Theresa Kapler told her friend,
"and living like we are is one of them.

Five years earlier, Theresa had no idea that she or
her family would ever get to such a point of desperation. In 1986 the Kapler family lived on an acre in the
country near Hawkeye, Iowa, a small town in the
northeast part of the state. Theresa stayed at home
with their two daughters, ages five and one, while
Rich worked for a construction company. They

attended mass every week, sometimes more than once. They were a normal, typical American family.

But all of that would change on a sunny fall day. That day little five-year-old Joy Kapler was mounted on a horse and allowed to sit on it as it walked on a field path through rows of dried cornstalks. Suddenly the animal spooked. When a horse spooks, it locks its legs and jerks sharply to the side to escape real or imagined danger. As the horse jerked to the left, Joy was thrown off to the right. Joy's body slammed down headfirst onto the black, hard soil of the field path. She blacked out momentarily and then regained consciousness.

After the accident Joy was stunned and dazed, and her eyes began rolling in her head. She vomited repeatedly and could not recall the accident or any of the events of the day. Richard and Theresa were horrified at what was happening to their beautiful, bright-eyed daughter.

"Your daughter has a concussion," the emergency room doctor told them after examining her. "You can take her home if you watch her carefully."

At home Joy began experiencing strange and painful symptoms. She had severe headaches and neck pain. She complained of a grid of lines "the color of white light" in her field of vision constantly. She often said, "Everything is fuzzy, Mamma, the TV, my dolly's face and your face." She cried mournfully, saying, "Nothing is the same."

Dizziness, lightheadedness, vomiting for no apparent reason and loss of balance plagued her. She lost her appetite. She was stiff and sore in her neck and had difficulty moving it. She experienced shooting pains in her arms and legs. Many times she cried out, "Mamma, my legs are going numb." Then her legs would collapse, and she would crumple to the floor.

Theresa and Rich took Joy to a long succession of doctors and chiropractors. Within a four-and-a-half year period, they went to fifty-six different professionals. These doctors used the following terms in describing her condition:

- injuries to the neck and upper back
- torn ligaments between cervical vertebrae
- traumatic cervical and thoracic strain and sprain aggravated by brain concussion
- torn ligaments and hypermobile motor units with headaches and blurred vision
- severe rotational and translational acceleration of the skull mass
- possible brain hemorrhage
- probable permanent eye damage
- disorientation
- retrograde and anterograde amnesia
- chronic post-traumatic bilateral cervical and cervical cranial radiculoneuropathies
- permanent physical impairment

All this was diagnosed within the first year and a half after the accident. The worst news was yet to come. Eventually Joy was referred to an expert in neurology and central nervous system management. Following painful and frightening tests, the doctor said Joy also had:

- traumatic brain injury

- damage to the temporal frontal lobes, left and right
- seizure disorder (partial complex seizures)
- migraine syndrome
- episodic difficulty with speech articulation and word finding
- episodic confusion
- partial loss of smell and taste

One doctor explained the magnitude of Joy's injury this way: "The daughter you had is dead, but that's not the worst news. The worst news is that you have to care for the one you have left." Rich and Theresa were stunned. What had happened to their outgoing talkative little girl?

Perhaps the long list of diagnoses is difficult to comprehend. Yet every item was a reality of life. One of the most disturbing problems was Joy's seizures. The first time one occurred, Joy was wide awake when suddenly her eyes went out of focus. She appeared to stare at nothing. "Joy, Joy, Joy," her mother shouted, waving her hand in front of her daughter's eyes. No response. Joy just sat and stared for several minutes.

The doctors identified these spells as partial complex seizures. "These are caused by scarring in the brain," doctors said. "When your daughter was thrown from the horse, ripping and tearing occurred deep in the brain. This damage often does not show up on any tests. But as these injuries tried to heal, scar tissue formed. Sometimes when the brain sends a signal it is interrupted by this scar tissue. Instead of taking its normal pathway, that brain wave shoots off into other areas of the brain. That is when unpredictable things

THIS IS YOUR DAY FOR A MIRACLE

happen in her body, mind and emotions."

Joy's neuropsychiatrist, known as one of the top in his field, explained that some cells of Joy's brain were completely nonfunctional. In addition, with each seizure, more brain cells were damaged or destroyed. Because medication could not bring the seizures completely under control, Joy continued to lose the use of more of her brain, "like fire kindling and burning inside a log, steadily consuming it."

Several EEG reports confirmed abnormal electrical activity in Joy's brain.

To the casual onlooker, Joy sometimes appeared fine, since she could walk around and talk clearly at times. The good days just served to make the bad days more depressing.

The team of doctors who monitored Joy described her as "chronically ill." The medical reports said the nine-year-old was "totally disabled" and "functionally illiterate."

Theresa pleaded with one doctor: "There has to be something, some way, some hope...."

He answered sternly, "You must come to understand and accept the fact that it is medically impossible for brain cells to regrow."

Watching Helplessly

Any parent knows that the hardest thing on earth is watching your child suffer. Joy suffered from her brain injury and other problems in complex and relentless ways.

The staring seizures were repeated with increasing frequency and variable duration.

Her memory functions were affected. One day

Joy's father was home for dinner. Joy talked with him as they ate dinner, and then Rich left the house again to go back to work. Shortly thereafter Joy asked her mother, "When is Daddy coming home to eat?" Joy experienced much confusion from her brain injury.

Her mother said, "Joy would rub her eyes severely. She would lose her memory of segments of time — sometimes hours, days or weeks. Her neuropsychiatrist said she would lose up to two weeks of time. During that time she walked and talked but later had no recollection of what had occurred." It was as if she were in a sleepwalking state.

The doctors decided the best course of treatment was to prescribe massive doses of Tegretol in an attempt to control the seizures. Inderal was prescribed to try to control the migraine headaches.

Migraine headaches were frequent. They caused vomiting and hallucinations. Often Joy cried out in frustration, "Mamma, there are red threads in the air everywhere. I can't see right. Help me!" She cried and kicked the chair or moaned and screamed in frustration and fear. Sometimes she panicked and talked about ants crawling on her arms, but there was nothing there.

In addition to everything else, Joy experienced sudden piercing pains in her eyes. One time Joy was in the kitchen when an eye pain hit. She screamed and backed up to a wall lined with cupboards. Then she pushed against the cupboards with her back and screamed again as she fell to the floor in pain.

The neuropsychiatrist said the eye pains felt like having an ice pick stuck in your eye. Medication had little effect on them. All that could be done in the worst cases was to give Joy a dose of Fiorinal that would knock her out.

Theresa remembered, "During those times Joy lay on the couch crying, 'Help me, Mamma. Help me!' She looked at me as if I had betrayed her. You know, at that age children think their mothers can fix anything." But Mother couldn't make the pain go away.

The pain of watching Joy go through this and not being able to do anything eventually caused Theresa to run out of the house and down the road when these attacks began, crying in her heart, "God, help us. Where are You, God, where?"

Yearning to Learn

Joy's accident occurred just as she was becoming school age. She had already learned some basics and showed above-average intelligence in her kindergarten round-up tests prior to the accident. But after her accident, Joy was not able to learn properly. According to her neurologist, the impact had damaged the part of her brain that allows a person to concentrate, focus, attend to things and be motivated.

Joy struggled with multiple learning disabilities. She had math dyslexia, which meant that the number *42* looked like *24*. She also had reading dyslexia, which caused the word *fish* to look like *hfis*. When she tried to speak, she sometimes pronounced words such as *cash register* as *rash cegister*. This caused Joy intense frustration and lowered self-esteem.

Instead of enjoying a normal childhood, she was a prisoner of her limitations. No longer a bubbly little girl, she became quiet and moody.

March 24, 1989

[redacted]
[redacted]
[redacted]
[redacted]

RE   Joy Kapler

Dear [redacted]

Thank you for your letter in late January concerning Joy.   I have
recently completed a long hospitalization and thorough re-evaluation
of Joy's situation. I feel that this child is totally disabled as a
result of minor motor seizures of the partial complex type, which
occur with a frequency of many times per week, with alterations in
awareness, despite very vigorous and rigorous therapy with medication
since March of 1988.   During these periods, the patient has an
impairment in communication, and between these periods, the patient
has difficulties with learning, difficulties with emotional lability,
and severe headaches that impair her school performance and which, in
fact, have required in-classroom aides to tutor the child several
hours per week.

Finally, this child has also developed significant depression and
psychological problems secondary to the recurrent seizures and head
injury which she has had. For this reason, I feel that she clearly has
emotional disorders that further impair her, although I would suggest
that we use the letter of [redacted], who has recently seen the
child in psychological consultation, to further support the detail in
this regard.

Sincerely,

[redacted signature]
[redacted]
[redacted]

This letter dated March 24, 1989, describes Joy's partial complex
seizures and the effects they had on her.

It's important to know that Joy's mental abilities varied from day to day. "It is like a vacuum cleaner with a frayed cord," one doctor said. "Sometimes it works and sometimes it doesn't. People will think she is normal because she acts so normal on good days."

When Joy was nine years old, an educational psychologist with eighteen years of experience spent an hour with her trying to teach her a phone number. With great effort he could help her remember three or four numbers in a row but within five minutes she would forget them.

Joy's educational outlook was poor. "She is pretty much left with molding clay," the educational consultants sadly concluded. At school Joy was placed in special education classes for the learning disabled.

A Depressed Daughter and Mother

Can you imagine how confusing the world was for Joy? In trying to deal with all of these problems she thought, "I can't do anything right." This beautiful little girl was depressed and insecure.

Theresa herself became suicidal after she finally accepted the fact that Joy would never improve. Theresa desperately wanted to hear from God. She continued to go to mass, but she also began visiting priests and even Protestant pastors, demanding, "Where is God now?"

One counselor told her, "All you have left is to make it to death." Others said, "God did this for a greater good in your life." Joy's mother began to hate a god who would do this to her little girl. She became resentful, bitter, hateful and cynical. Theresa

June 27, 1988

re: Joy Anna Kapler

Dear

    I saw Joy recently after about 2 hours on the phone with her mother in preliminary discussion. Obviously from your reports (and her mother's descriptions), the child has a seizure disorder. Unfortunately, Joy's mother tells me that her most recent tegretol level was in the 5 to 6 range, and that Joy had had a particualrly bad day with headaches on the day prior to my exam. Thus, I assume that I did not see the child at her best. I certainly hope so.

    Joy was tested by   in October of 1987, and the results of this exam were available to me when I saw Joy. Unforunately, Joy's WISC-R Full Scale IQ was 12 points worse for me than for   (112 vs. 100). Her dichotic listening was L=18/50, R=42/50, this despite the fact that she did not know the meaning of about a third of the words she repeated correctly in the right ear. At least as of today, she is functionally illiterate. On the positive side, she was able to engage in undirected constructive play for 30 minutes without adult supervision or attention.

    I believe that I should reexamine this child sometime two or three months after her tegretol levels have stabalized.

Best regards,

Joy's neuropsychologist describes her as "functionally illiterate" in this letter written when Joy was seven years old, two years after falling from a horse.

commented, "I now believe one of satan's greatest tricks is to defame or lie about the character of Jesus Christ and so set a person against the only hope who can help us. The Bible says satan — not God — comes to kill, rob and destroy, but Jesus came that we may have and enjoy life and have it in abundance" (see John 10:10).

In desperation Theresa began to read her Bible daily. The stories she read from her Bible were full of healing and victory. Yet all around her was defeat and hopelessness. Many times, not understanding, she slammed the Bible against the wall, shouting, "Why does it say *this* in here? My life is not like this."

Family Deterioration

The other family members were also sucked down into the whirlpool of hopelessness. By 1989, with the recommendation of specialists, Joy was taken out of the public school system. Theresa attempted to home-school Joy with the help of an educational consultant who specialized in rehabilitation from closed head injuries. The consultant noted, "Reading a simple sentence was painful, almost agonizing. Yet she did well on her IQ test except on things involving memory and attention span." As a result, Joy was aware that she should be able to do better at her schoolwork, but found herself unable to do so.

Meanwhile a typical day for Rich consisted of getting up at 5 A.M. to go to his job as a carpenter. When he returned home late in the evening, he and Theresa stayed up talking, sometimes until 2 A.M. "The doctors have nothing good to say. I can't believe this is happening. What are we going to do?"

October 24, 1989

FOLLOW-UP FOR
Joy Kapler

Unfortunately, very bad results have been returned on Joy's educational abilities at this time. She basically has a very poor educational outlook, with very poor test performances, mainly secondary to frontal lobe symptomatology, with difficulty with motivation, impulse control, insight, planning, etc. These are rather typical findings in this setting. She is also having increased difficulties with her headaches and seizure symptoms, including staring spells again.

We will increase her Tegretol to 400-300-300-500, obtain a new level, CBC, and SGOT in a week, and increase her Inderal to 160 mg LA PO QAM and 80 mg LA PO QHS. We will follow-up in one month by phone.

(Dictated but not read by)

In this follow-up note, Joy's neurologist described the problems that Joy suffered after her fall in 1986.

Piles of bills mounted up from every direction. Rich often sat at his desk rubbing his forehead. "I felt overwhelmed and had no hope that we could ever overcome all those bills," Rich related. "I didn't put my trust in God and tried to carry it all myself. I felt frustrated, alone, fearful and inadequate up against it all."

Rich became depressed and withdrawn and began to avoid conversation with Theresa, sometimes for days, weeks or months on end. "I didn't know how to fix it all or what decisions to make any more, and I was just running away from it all," Rich related.

Counselors had earlier told Rich and Theresa that 89 percent of those who have a child with the severity of Joy's impairment end up divorced. "That will never happen to us," they vowed, but now they were on the verge of divorce.

Kelsey, Joy's sister, was a one-year-old at the time of the accident. She grew up in a home with little laughter and little time for her. Kelsey started having symptoms of asthma around the same time as Joy's accident, and the emotional stress of the home made it even worse. By 1990 Kelsey's asthma was so bad that she had to be hooked up to a breathing machine for at least twenty minutes every four hours — day and night — to clear her airways. She also took Ventolin syrup.

During this time, God sent a woman into Theresa's life. This woman wasn't a doctor or a pastor. She was a Christian who believed the Word of God. She told Theresa, "God doesn't want you to suffer. Jesus wants to heal Joy."

Theresa thought she was crazy.

The Turning Point

By the fall of 1990, four years after the accident, the Kapler family was worn out. Theresa often thought to herself, "One bullet would get me out of all this."

On October 24, 1990, Theresa agonized as Joy lay on the couch suffering from an eye pain. Suddenly she bolted out of the door of the house and ran into the cornfields. She ran for miles until she fell down in between the corn rows with her face in the dirt, utterly exhausted, without the will to go on for even one more hour.

"God," she cried in her heart, "I have tried to be a good soldier. There's nothing left — nothing. If You don't take my life now, I will." She was so depressed and exhausted that she told God she would not get up ever again, even if she rotted on that spot on the ground. At this point, at the end of all self-effort and at the end of any ability in herself to carry on with life, God revealed Himself (see John 14:21).

Theresa remembered, "I felt an invisible power raise me up to a kneeling position. I knew it was the Lord. Then the clouds moved and parted, and I beheld the face of Jesus. Tears poured out of my eyes. I had not cried in over two years. Resurrection life, love, joy and peace seemed to flow through my entire being. There are no words to describe the glory of God. I knew in an instant that God was real, that He was on my side, and that He didn't bring this misery into my life."

After Theresa walked home from the cornfield, she immediately called her Christian friend, the one she *used* to think was crazy.

"You won't believe what happened to me!" she

exclaimed. "I want what you have," she told her friend.

The woman came to the Kaplers' house and led Theresa, Joy and Kelsey in prayer to receive Jesus as their Savior and to receive the baptism of the Holy Spirit (see John 3:3; Acts 1:5).

They prayed, "Lord Jesus, I give up. I quit. I can't put it together. Come into my heart, and take over my life. God, forgive me for all my sins and cleanse me by Your blood. I ask You to fill me with Your Holy Spirit, and I surrender the rest of my life to You. I call upon You to save, deliver and heal us" (see Mark 11:23-24).

Immediately Theresa had an insatiable hunger for God's Word. She read ravenously, feeding on the Word like a hungry animal and understanding it in a way she never had before.

Two weeks later there was a healing service at a meeting of the Full Gospel Businessmen's Association in a nearby town. The night of the meeting it was pouring down rain and Theresa had never been to a FGBA meeting, but she put both her daughters in the car and went.

The speaker gave a simple testimony of God's power. He had been delivered from an addiction to drugs and did not go through withdrawal. His wife had been delivered from drinking a fifth of Black Velvet liquor a day. Theresa was surprised and wondered, "How can this be? This isn't possible."

When an invitation for prayer was given Theresa said she "almost walked right over" the woman between her and the aisle, dragging both daughters with her. The speaker prayed with Kelsey to be delivered of asthma and for Joy to be healed. When he got to Theresa, she asked that he pray for her marriage to be healed, for healing of pain and stiffness in her joints and for an end to her anger. He prayed and then led Theresa in a prayer of forgiveness.

"I let go of all the hatred, unforgiveness, bitterness and resentment I had in my heart," Theresa said, "and now I know this was a major turning point in our lives. I believe it opened the door for the miracles that occurred that night, for the healing of our marriage and eventually for Joy's miracle."

On the way home, Theresa noticed that Kelsey didn't cough. That night Kelsey slept without coughing, something she had not done for many months before. When Theresa went in to put her on the breathing machine, Kelsey was sleeping and breathing so well that she had peace about skipping the treatment.

In the morning, Theresa woke up feeling better than she had ever felt in her life. As she got out of bed, she thought about the pain she experienced in her joints, which was worst in the mornings. She usually had to grip the handrail and proceed slowly just to get down the stairs in the mornings. That morning, she said, "It felt as if I floated down the stairs." All symptoms were gone! Theresa could hardly believe what had happened to her. She had once mocked and persecuted those who believed in healing.

Since that evening of November 2, 1990, Kelsey has had no more symptoms of asthma. She was eventually taken off all medication for her asthma and has never needed or used the breathing machine again.

Joy's condition remained virtually the same, but

other changes were happening in the family that would profoundly affect her.

By this time Theresa began to pray for her husband. As she did, she was filled with supernatural love for him. Two weeks into November, Rich sent Theresa, Joy and Kelsey a Thanksgiving card saying that he loved them. On Thanksgiving Day, Rich came to the house for dinner. After four hours he finally burst out, "Theresa, what has happened to you?"

"Why do you ask?" Theresa replied, afraid he wouldn't understand if she told him.

"I have been in this house four hours now and you haven't been angry once. What has happened to you?" By the end of the evening Rich told her, "I want what you have." Two days later he was born again and filled with the Holy Spirit. He began to read the Bible daily. God changed his life in many significant ways and restored his and Theresa's marriage.

Empowered to Fight

A friend loaned Theresa a copy of my book, *Good Morning, Holy Spirit,* during this time when she began to wage the battle for Joy's healing. Theresa began to read about the Person of the Holy Spirit through this book and learn how to fellowship with Him. Each morning when she first woke up or was straightening the bed, she would greet the Holy Spirit.

"This is what I was hungering for all my life," Theresa said. "No one can fill the emptiness in a person except for God. There's no satisfaction, adventure or excitement like communicating with and being led by the Person of the Holy Spirit of the living God."

Theresa did not have Christian television in her

home. But a friend made videotapes for her of *This Is Your Day!* and other programs where I preached. Theresa said that hearing about the healings and receiving the teaching was like an oasis in the desert for her. The programs amazed her because she had never seen anything like them before.

Theresa was inspired to wage spiritual warfare for Joy's healing, but felt so exhausted and alone, that she thought she was losing the battle.

Then one day her Christian friend told her, "Someone wants to pay your way to go to a Christian conference in Minneapolis. Do you want to go?" Theresa jumped at the chance.

This special conference was Invasion '91, hosted by Roberts Liardon. I was to teach some sessions at the conference and conduct a miracle crusade on August 29 and 30.

In one session I spoke about surrender. This precious daughter of God said that it was then that she gave up spiritual pride. Before she was born again, she thought she knew all about God, having gone to church all her life. When she encountered the living God in person, she realized she had only just begun the journey of knowing Him.

At one of the sessions where I taught, Theresa and Joy sat together. I didn't notice them in the crowd, but Jesus did. I gave an invitation, "If you want to serve God with all of your heart, come up here."

Theresa came forward in a huge crowd of people. I prayed for the power of God to touch them. Theresa remembered, "The power of God came on me, and I fell backward. For some time I was pinned to the floor, unable to get up."

Theresa left the crusade filled with the power of God. She prayed loudly and boldly in the Spirit during the four-hour drive home in the car with her two daughters. When she arrived home, she marched through her house for hours, praying. In the spirit she felt like a warrior shouting to satan, "It is finished. Jesus is the victor!" She began to see the demonic forces that had gained entry into her household.

Finishing the Battle

Soon after, Theresa was washing dishes when Joy came to her and said, "I don't feel good." Joy had another migraine headache. "Let's pray," Theresa said and laid her hands on Joy's head.

She prayed, "I bind the power of satan and all evil spirits, and I command you to go in Jesus' name. I praise God for the victory. I loose the protection of the blood of Jesus and an angel. I loose an infilling of the Holy Spirit in Jesus' name."

Joy looked up at her mother with surprise, "It's gone!" she said. The migraine went away instantly. They didn't have to fight in prayer all day as they had before.

Every time Joy experienced pain or other symptoms, Theresa laid hands on her and prayed. Where the prayers seemed to have had limited effect before, they were now powerful. Migraines went away. Eye pains stopped.

Theresa continued to bathe Joy in prayer for a complete healing, being sensitive to the Holy Spirit to guide her. One time she and her daughters had been reading the Bible and praying for hours and then went to the kitchen. Joy had crackers in her hand, and she was eating. Theresa felt at that moment that she should pray for Joy, so she simply laid her hands on her head and prayed.

To her amazement, Theresa saw in her spirit "a funnel of white light, narrowing, coming down like rays and into Joy's head like a bomb of radiant glory and fire." A few minutes later she saw another cylinder of white light go into Joy's head, down through her back and spine and out her feet. Joy stayed rooted to the ground for the next twenty minutes as the glory of God surged through her.

That day Theresa knew that God had done something astounding for Joy.

One day Joy called for her mother with a serious look on her face. "Mamma, I'm going to tell you a story," she said.

Though Joy often had a hard time speaking, let alone telling a story, Theresa wanted to be sensitive to her daughter. "OK," she said. "You tell it, and I'll write."

"The name of the story is 'Teddy Bear in Trouble,'" Joy began. Then she told the story of a teddy bear who couldn't do anything right anymore and didn't understand why. Her mother could not help her. Then the teddy bear realized that there was only one who could help her — Jesus. Then Jesus came and got the teddy bear out of trouble.

Theresa was shocked and dumbfounded — not only at the story but at the fact that Joy put all the sentences together and sequenced the events of the story. What was God doing?

Some time later, Joy came to her mother with

another unusual comment. "Mamma, write some numbers for me." Theresa took a pencil and some paper and wrote four numbers in a row.

"Write some more," Joy said.

Theresa patiently carried out the request, finally writing a column of four numbers with four digits each. It would have looked like this:

$$4572$$
$$2401$$
$$1005$$
$$7439$$

Joy pulled the pencil out of her mother's hand and began adding the numbers together. She wrote her answer beneath the numbers and pushed the paper toward her mother. Theresa stared in shock. Joy had added the four numbers together and written the correct answer.

Remember, on many days Joy could not recall the answer to 2 + 2. Her memory loss and math dyslexia had been recognized by educational psychologists. Joy had never done or learned anything like this before in her life.

Theresa remembered, "When she added up those numbers and got the correct answer, I was overwhelmed with stark, cold fear of God's awesome power. I was terrified. How had God done this? Joy handed me the pencil and looked at me. I threw the pencil across the room and ran upstairs taking two steps at a time until I got to the bathroom. I slammed the door shut and locked it behind me. God was so close, and His presence so powerful that it was as if I were trying to hide from Him. I went to the window and leaned on the sill, crying and whispering over and over, 'My Lord and my God. My Lord and my God.'"

Victory!

Joy was still taking high levels of strong medication, and she frequently went to a local clinic for blood draws. The results of the blood tests were sent to the neurologist who was regulating Joy's dosage of Tegretol, the drug that was prescribed for her seizures. The doctor's goal was to keep the amount of medicine in Joy's bloodstream at the highest possible level in an attempt to control the seizures. Yet he discovered that Joy was requiring less and less of the drug.

On November 21, 1991, within three months after attending the teaching sessions and crusade, Joy began a new life — medication free.

Not only that — Joy was free from the eye pains, free from the migraines and free from the seizures. She was free to learn and remember and live again.

"It was months before anyone could laugh or cry," Theresa explained. "It was like we were all in shock. Medically there was no way Joy could have been healed without a creative miracle to her brain. The Creator is still creating and recreating" (see Heb. 13:8).

The Kapler home was filled with the reverent awe and wonder of God. They spent much time in praise, deep worship and reading God's Word.

In February it was time for Joy's yearly educational evaluation. An educational psychologist who had administered progress tests to Joy for the past several years agreed to visit the Kapler home to administer the tests. He had seen Joy the previous year and concurred that she was functionally illiterate and faced great challenges in learning.

Instead of taking the normal hour to administer the test, the doctor spent more than three hours with Joy. Earlier Theresa had warned him, "Listen, God has done a miracle."

"Oh, I believe you," he replied.

When he was finished, he called Theresa into the room. His face was ashen white and the first words he spoke were, "This is not the same girl. What has happened here?"

Joy did math problems she had never done before. She tested well in humanities, reading comprehension and science. To top it off, she could easily remember six to seven numbers in sequence.

The doctor insisted on knowing what happened, so Theresa told him the story of Joy's healing and her salvation. Immediately he wanted to receive Jesus. Theresa led him in the prayer of salvation, and he prayed to receive the baptism of the Holy Spirit. This same doctor gave Joy several more tests over the next two years. He finally concluded, "In nineteen years as a psychologist, I have never seen such improvement."

This professional was one of many who grew in faith through the miracle of the Kapler family.

Joy's neurologist said of her recovery: "This is a resurrection from the living dead! This shows clear-cut, superhuman intervention." Joy's neurologist sees many patients with traumatic brain injury, seizure disorder and migraine syndrome. He was once offered a position at Baylor College of Medicine in Houston,

June 17, 1993

To whom it may concern:

I have provided psychological and educational services for Joy Kapler and her family for over five years. I witnessed the suffering and frustration of this youngster as she struggled to maintain her attention and remember simple bits of information only to fail repeatedly. I can testify that her educational progress had practically come to a standstill as a result of her brain injury.

A little over a year after her healing I was invited by Theresa and Richard Kapler to once again work with Joy and assess her educational progress. To put it mildly, I was astonished and amazed at her progress educationally, but her concentration and memory improvements were beyond description! I have never seen a youngster recover these lost abilities and can think of no natural process by which they can be renewed. Each time I am around Joy now I marvel at the progress she has made and the peace she radiates since her healing.

Although Joy lost ground educationally during the years of her disability, she is making progress that would have been impossible prior to her healing. In every other way Joy appears to be a normal, happy, healthy child who has been blessed by God's healing power, and she shows it!

_____

November 23, 1992

To whom it may concern:

I want to verify that I administered a number of psychological tests to Joy Kapler at the time she was experiencing some of her most severe learning, attention span, memory, and emotional problems resulting from her brain injury. I also administered tests and observed her behavior following her healing. From a psychological perspective she is not the same girl. Her memory problems have disappeared, her attention span is now normal or better, her learning of basic academic subjects is now progressing at the expected rate, and she is quite obviously a much happier and emotionally healthier child following her healing. In nineteen years as a psychologist I have never seen such improvement. This child now has an inner peace which, thought it cannot be measured by any psychological test, is obvious to everyone around her.

Sincerely,

School and Licensed Psychologist

The above letters from the psychologist who worked with Joy verify the dramatic change in her abilities and progress after she received her healing.

Texas, a leading neurological institute. He now publishes and lectures nationally on the subject of head injury.

In the summer of 1995, this neurologist stated during an interview for national radio that prior to Joy's miracle he had been a Christian, but he did not believe in miracles. Now he not only believes in miracles, but has even referred some of his patients to the Kaplers for prayer.

Friends, family members and people across America surrendered their lives to Jesus as they saw the change in Joy. Others contacted the family after reading about the story in newspapers and magazines. It was printed in seven secular Northeast Iowa newspapers, reported on two local secular television stations and featured in five magazines with worldwide circulation. It has also been translated into Chinese by a neurologist in Taiwan who then published it in *Chinese Missions Magazine*. The Kaplers were also interviewed twice on *The 700 Club*.

The family now actively ministers to hurting people in desperate situations. Theresa said, "I can't walk by the man in the ditch anymore." Healings and miracles take place through their prayers (see Mark 16:17-18).

"How God loves His people! He hungers for them," Theresa explained. "He calls on the church to bring Him the lost, hurting, broken, desperate and dying because Jesus is coming (Matt. 24:14). The end-time harvest is ripe. When we come to Him with all our hearts, the Lord brings deliverance, healing and restoration to homes, health and relationships (2 Chr. 7:14). Lay aside disobedience, unforgiveness and unbelief and receive all the promises of God's Word."

[blurred letterhead]

July 12, 1993

RE: Joy Kapler

To Whom It May Concern:

This is a resurrection from the living dead. This shows clear-cut superhuman intervention. Let the world be informed we have grown in faith through the miracle of a little girl.

[signature]

[name, blurred]

Board Certified Neurologist

[blurred line]

"A resurrection from the living dead" are the neurologist's exact words. Here he tells of how he and others have grown in faith because of Joy Kapler's miracle.

Joy Kapler Today

What is Joy Kapler like today? She is a healthy, peaceful fifteen-year-old. She is home-schooled by her mother using Christian curriculum. Reading and history are her favorite subjects. She takes piano lessons and plays the tambourine during the family worship time.

She begins every day reading the Word of God and enjoys watching *This Is Your Day!* because people on the show tell about miracles and healings God has done for them. She travels with her family to churches, clubs and organizations as they tell of God's saving, healing, delivering power and love. They often pray together for the sick and hurting.

The first time Joy told her miracle story was to a little girl who had leukemia. They were on their way to a healing service when Joy told the girl about the Bible story where a sick man's friends tore the roof apart trying to get their friend to Jesus. "That's what we're doing for you now," Joy told the girl. Joy's friend is alive and healthy today.

Joy still has a hard time talking about her life before she was healed. The painful memories bring tears. She said, "I had a lot of headaches and a lot of pain. I couldn't do schoolwork. It was hard. For math I couldn't remember the stuff I should remember."

Her favorite verse is Exodus 15:26: "For I am the Lord who healeth thee" (KJV). She says there is one thing everyone should know: "There's nothing too big that God can't do. He can heal anybody and do anything."

Lessons From
the Great Physician

It happened that as he made his way toward Jerusalem, he crossed over the border between Samaria and Galilee. As he entered a village, ten men, all lepers, met him. They kept their distance but raised their voices, calling out, "Jesus, Master, have mercy on us!"

Taking a good look at them, he said, "Go, show yourselves to the priests."

They went, and while still on their way, became clean. One of them, when he realized that he was healed, turned around and came back, shouting his gratitude, glorifying God. He kneeled at Jesus' feet, so grateful. He couldn't thank him enough — and he was a Samaritan.

Jesus said, "Were not ten healed? Where are the nine? Can none be found to come back and give glory to God except this outsider?" Then he said to him. "Get up. On your way. Your faith has healed and saved you."

Luke 17:11-19

One of them, when he realized that
he was healed turned around and came back,
shouting his gratitude, glorifying God.

13

The Key to
Your Miracle

I AM CONSTANTLY asked, "Pastor Benny, why are some people healed and others are not?"

As you have read the inspiring accounts of people like Jerry Wood, Patricia Harrington, Ray Scott and Brenda Forgy, perhaps you have pondered the same question. Did they have a level of faith that was far above average. Did they do something special to receive God's favor?

Recently, in a meeting we conducted at the Anaheim Convention Center in California, the platform was lined with people who were praising God for the miracles they received.

During that service my attention was repeatedly drawn to a beautiful little girl in a wheelchair. I prayed, "Lord, please heal that girl. Please heal her."

As the final song was being sung and the service was about to conclude, I looked in her direction again. She was still there — confined to that wheelchair.

Believe me, if I had the power to heal, that girl would not have left the building as she came. I continue to pray for her, believing one day she will walk again. But healing is the work of God, not of man.

More Faith?

I remember Kathryn Kuhlman often talking about how she wrestled with this topic. She was greatly disturbed when a minister would tell someone who was desperately ill, "You are not being healed because you don't have enough faith!"

With great emotion, she expressed how her heart ached for these people because she knew how they struggled, day after day, trying desperately to obtain *more* faith. "They were analyzing the faith they had," she said, "in a hopeless effort to discover the deficiency which was presumably keeping them from the healing power of God. And I knew the inevitability of their defeat, because they were looking at themselves rather than to God."

The answer cannot be found in yourself. Faith cannot be self-produced. It is not the result of your goodness, your morality, your benevolence or your service. And since it is not of human origin, it cannot be produced by your mind.

I believe faith is more than hope or expectation.

Faith is alive because of a person. His name is Jesus.

It is really quite simple. Where Christ is present, faith is present. Where Christ is absent, faith is absent.

Kathryn Kuhlman often told the story of Jesus crossing the Sea of Galilee with His disciples in a small boat. A terrific storm arose and the disciples were frightened. The boat was about to capsize and they would surely drown. They awakened Christ and said, "Master, master, we perish" (Luke 8:24, KJV).

Jesus arose and rebuked the wind. The raging waters were suddenly calm. Then He asked the disciples, "Where is your faith?"

After telling the story, Miss Kuhlman asked these questions about the disciples' faith: "Where was it? Had they left it on shore before entering the boat? Had it dropped to the depth of the sea on which their little boat was sailing? Had it fled on the shoulders of the storm?"

She concluded, "Their faith had been resting in the stern of the boat! Their faith was with them all the time — it had never left them for one second. *Jesus* was their faith."

Jesus meant it when He said, "Without me ye can do nothing" (John 15:5, KJV). Faith in Jesus is the only faith you need. Remember, trust and belief are not of yourself; they are centered in Christ and you must move toward Him. He declared, "Come unto me all ye that labour and are heavy laden, and I will give you rest" (Matt. 11:28, KJV).

Why Does Christ Heal?

Scripture records many miracles performed by

Christ. Scripture also shows us why Jesus still heals today.

1. Jesus heals because He has compassion.

Because of what He endured on the cross, the Lord fully understands the pain and suffering we experience. "For we have not an high priest which cannot be touched with the feelings of our infirmities" (Heb. 4:15, KJV).

A man with leprosy came to the Lord one day and said, "If you are willing, you can make me clean." Jesus was filled with compassion for this man. Scripture says He touched him and said, "I am willing. Be clean!" (Mark 1:40-41, KJV).

The moment Jesus spoke those words the leprosy departed. He was healed!

2. Jesus heals to bring glory to His Father.

Christ knew the source of His power and continually reminded people that He had come to do the work of His Father (John 5:19-20, KJV).

Once when the Lord Jesus was near the Sea of Galilee, "Great crowds came to him, bringing the lame, the blind, the crippled, the dumb and many others, and laid them at his feet; and he healed them" (Matt. 15:30, NIV).

When the people saw the tremendous miracles taking place "they praised the God of Israel" (v. 31, NIV).

On another occasion, when Jesus heard that Lazarus of Bethany was sick, He proclaimed, "This sickness is not unto death, but for the glory of God, that the Son of God may be glorified through it" (John 11:4, NKJV).

3. Jesus heals to fulfill the Father's promise.

The miracles of Christ — in New Testament times and today — are the fulfillment of God's promises spoken through His prophets to us His people.

When Christ came to Peter's house, Scripture records, "Many who were demon-possessed were brought to him, and he drove out the spirits with a word and healed all the sick. This was to fulfill what was spoken through the prophet Isaiah: 'He took up our infirmities and carried our diseases'" (Matt. 8:16-17, NIV).

4. Healing belongs to His children.

A Canaanite woman whose little daughter was possessed by an evil spirit heard that Jesus was coming to her town. She came and fell at His feet, begging Him to heal her daughter. The Scripture goes on to tell of the dialogue between her and the Lord. This dialogue seems perplexing at first, but if you really look at it, two beautiful truths emerge.

In answer to her request for healing, Jesus told the woman, "Let the children first be filled." With those words, Jesus acknowledged that healing is a gift God gives to His children.

Unfortunately, the woman who stood before Christ was not considered a "child of God" at the time. She was a Gentile. In metaphor, Jesus explained, "...it is not good to take the children's bread and throw it to the dogs."

But the woman persisted, "Yes, Lord, yet even the little dogs under the table eat from the children's crumbs."

To this Jesus responded, "For this saying go your way; the demon has gone out of your daughter."

In Jesus' response we see that God heals without respect of persons.

5. Healing demonstrates the power of God.

In Jerusalem, when the critics of Christ came against Him, He answered them, "Do not believe me unless I do what my Father does. But if I do it, even though you do not believe me, believe the miracles, that you may learn and understand that the Father is in me, and I in the Father" (John 10:37-38, NIV).

6. Healing demonstrates the power of His blood.

I never conduct a service without thanking Christ for His blood. Every time I do, the presence of God descends and miracles begin taking place. When we thank the Lord for His sacrifice on the cross and acknowledge the work of the cross, it is then that the Holy Spirit descends and touches people's lives.

Why does this happen? Christ's death on the cross was not only for your salvation, but for your healing. What God inspired the prophet Isaiah to write is still true: "Surely He has borne our griefs and carried our sorrows; yet we esteemed Him stricken, smitten by God, and afflicted. But he was wounded for our transgressions, he was bruised for our iniquities; the chastisement for our peace was upon Him; and by His stripes we are healed" (Is. 53:4-5, NKJV).

7. Jesus heals to destroy the works of the devil.

Every time someone is healed, satan is dealt a

devastating blow. Scripture declares, "For this purpose the Son of God was manifested, that He might destroy the works of the devil" (1 John 3:8, NKJV).

Scripture shows Jesus' authority over satan by telling of the many times where the Lord cast out demons during His ministry on earth (Mark 1:24-26; Luke 11:14). One time the Pharisees accused Him of casting out demons by satan's power. Jesus rebuked them and clearly showed that He came to overcome the work of satan.

> If I cast out demons by Beelzebub, by whom do your sons cast them out? Therefore they will be your judges. But if I cast out demons with the finger of God, surely the kingdom of God has come upon you. When a strong man, fully armed, guards his own palace, his goods are in peace. But when a stronger than he comes upon him and overcomes him, he takes from him all his armor in which he trusted, and divides his spoils (Luke 11:19-22, NKJV).

What Is the Answer?

I told a fellow minister in Florida recently, "I have to believe in miracles. I have no choice. With the sin and sickness I see in our world, I doubt I could face another day if I did not believe God can intervene in the lives of man."

Because God heals there is always hope. Recently I spoke with the father of a girl who was dying. The moment he knew I was going to pray for his daughter he said, "You don't know what this means to me. Now I can go to work today." It was hope that gave him the ability to go forward.

People continually ask me, "What can I do to receive my miracle?

"Nothing," I tell them.

Healing is not a result of what we do. It is a result of what Christ has *already done.*

God sent His Son to die on the cross to guarantee your salvation and make a way for your healing.

This is the source of all hope. You can get up and go on because Christ has given eternal life to *every* person who believes in Him. No sickness, heartache, pain or even death can take that away.

Always remember, Jesus knows every pain you feel. He hears your cries and His heart is full of mercy for you. In His sovereign grace, that moment will come when He will say, "This is your day for a miracle!"

Bless the Lord, O my soul:
And all that is within me, bless His holy name!
Bless the Lord, O my soul,
And forget not all His benefits:
Who forgives all your iniquities,
Who heals all your diseases,
Who redeems your life from destruction,
Who crowns you with lovingkindness and tender
  mercies,
Who satisfies your mouth with good things,
So that your youth is renewed like the eagle's (Ps.
  103:1-5, NKJV).

Editor's Note

The people whose stories appear in
this book have given Creation House
written permission to use their stories
and to reproduce medical records and
photos regarding their cases.

The names of medical professionals
have been withheld from the stories and
blurred out in medical documents
in order to protect their privacy. Other
blurred items on medical records
include comments of a personal nature
and names of hospitals, clinics and
insurance companies.

Other Teaching Materials by Benny Hinn

The following books and audiocassettes by Benny Hinn are also available from the World Outreach Center or from your local Christian bookstore:

The Blood
Good Morning, Holy Spirit
The Anointing
Welcome, Holy Spirit

The Anointing (audiocassette)
The Blood (audiocassette)
Good Morning, Holy Spirit (audiocassette)

If you experience a miracle as a result of reading this book, please bless us by telling us about it.
Contact:

World Outreach Center
7601 Forest City Road
Orlando, FL 32810-1499
407-293-7449

The Power of the Blood Study Series

Now your Sunday school class, home group Bible
study and your family can experience
the revelation of the shed blood of Jesus Christ.

The Blood
by Benny Hinn
Benny Hinn introduces you to the power for daily
living in the blood of Jesus. From Genesis to Jesus to
you, Hinn examines the importance of the blood
covenant and how it is the source of power, protection and promise for you today.

The Power of the Blood Video
In this extraordinary video, taped live on location
in Israel, Benny Hinn teaches about the wonder-
working power of Jesus' shed blood. This great
learning device goes hand in hand with the
new eight-week study guide.

The Power of the Blood Study Guide
This eight-week interactive study guide helps
individuals and small groups or classes to
understand how the biblical teachings about the
blood of Jesus can powerfully touch
and transform lives.

For more information call 1-800-283-8494

The Church Home Pak

The Church Home Pak includes Benny Hinn's best-selling book *The Blood*, plus *The Power of the Blood* study guide and the *Power of the Blood* video, all in one convenient package.

For more information call 1-800-283-8494